In this classic work by T. Austin Sparks, the author brings us back to the central focus of our faith . . . the Cross.

Without this focus Christianity becomes a muddled combination of distorted doctrines and half truths.

If you understand the Cross, then you will understand the eternal purpose of God himself!

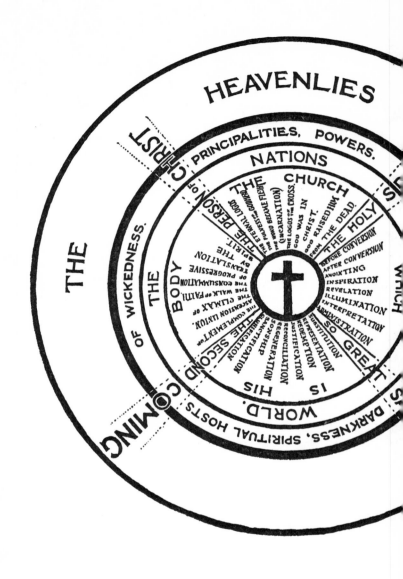

THE REALITY
OF THE
CROSS OF CHRIST

by

T. AUSTIN-SPARKS

"FAR ABOVE ALL"

Barbour and Company, Inc.
164 Mill Street
Westwood, NJ

ISBN 1-55748-013-3

Published by: **BARBOUR AND COMPANY, INC.**
164 Mill Street
Westwood, New Jersey 07675

EVANGELICAL CHRISTIAN PUBLISHERS ASSOCIATION 🄴🄲🄿🄰 MEMBER

This book was previously published under the title
The Centrality and Universality of the Cross

Printed in the United States of America

CONTENTS

Introductory

THE Bible—when we stand back and view it as a whole—gives us two views of the universe. Firstly there is the standpoint of eternity and of God's eternal purpose. From this the universe is Christo-centric. Secondly there is the standpoint of the incursion of sin, with all its effects. From this point of view the universe is Redempto-centric. The former represents the tremendous significance of Jesus Christ, Son of God and Son of man. The latter sets forth the terrible and glorious meaning of Jesus Christ and Him crucified; in other words, the Cross. It is with this second, as with the wheel within the greater wheel, that we are now occupied. The greater has become wholly dependent upon the other, and so the Cross becomes adorned with all the significance of the universal purpose of God from eternity to eternity.

In order to meet any misconception as to unbalanced emphasis, let us once and for all say that, according to the revelation of the entire Word of God, both in the Old and New Testaments, the Cross is now basic to everything, and the diagram which is before you (see inset) represents a wheel with all its spokes and its rim, and its wheels within wheels, but the hub of everything is the Cross of the Lord Jesus. It is not one of the spokes; it is not one of the lines of teaching; but it gathers up in itself everything, and it makes possible everything. If you fail to recognize God's place and God's meaning for and in the Cross of the Lord Jesus, it is then that you become unbalanced; you become departmental, your perspective is thrown out and your vision is distorted. For the right adjustment and regulation and balancing of all truth you must place the Cross right at the centre and see the relationship of everything else to it, and of it to everything else.

We venture to say that there is not a theme in all the Word of God relative to the eternal purpose of God which is not governed by the Cross of the Lord Jesus. In the smallest matters of practical everyday life, the Cross is to have its place, and from commonplace things the application is to be made to ever widening circles.

Of course, it is understood that the phrase "the Cross" does not merely mean the crucifixion of Christ, but the death, the burial, the resurrection and ascension to the throne, and the sovereign relationship vested now in Christ there for us; all is by way of the Cross. We never see the throne apart from the Lamb in the midst thereof "as though it had been slain." Everything is gathered up in the phrase: " Jesus Christ and him crucified," and when " the Cross " is mentioned, " Christ crucified " with all that that implies is meant.

So then, let us recognize once and for all, that the Cross is not a specific line of teaching, not a department of truth, not an isolated message in an unbalanced emphasis, but the all-comprehending, all-explaining centre of the universe. It is the hub of the wheel. To it and from it all the spokes move through clearly defined circles of Divine instrumentality and activity unto the farthest bound of the universe; in the super-heavenlies, the heavenlies " far above all ": there the Cross is still. You never get outside of the range of the Cross.

Having said that the Cross is not a phase of truth, but is now the centre or hub of all the truth—the basis, the issue, and the explanation of everything—we shall now proceed to see how that is so in relation to the four major lines of revelation as to Christ. These four ' spokes ' moving out from the hub and ever coming back to it are:

    I.   The Person of Christ.
    II.   The Holy Spirit.
   III.   The So Great Salvation.
   IV.   The Coming again of the Lord.

CHAPTER I.

The Cross and the Person of Christ

It is of far-reaching importance and vital consequence to recognise that the Person of our Lord cannot really be known and understood apart from the Cross. It is equally of consequence to realise that the Cross is only really understood and adequately appreciated when the Person of Christ is discerned. These two work hand-in-hand and are mutually dependent.

Who Jesus Is

In the days of His earthly life His disciples and the people wanted a Crossless Christ. They could see no place for the Cross. It was a contradiction of all their hopes and expectations. Whenever He referred to it a dark shadow crept over them, and they were offended. Indeed, they revolted quite positively against the idea and suggestion.

Running parallel to this inability to discern the meaning and the value of the Cross was, on the one hand, His continual reference to His own essential Person as Son of God, and on the other hand, their total inability to recognise Him. Only in fleeting flashes of illumination did one or two of them see Him as such, and then, it would seem from their behaviour, that they lost the realisation, and the general clouds of uncertainty wrapt them around again. The state and position in which we find them when He has been crucified indicates how the reality of His Person had failed to possess their innermost life. But the interesting and significant thing is that the Lord all the time indicated that this twofold inability would be removed when actually the Cross was an accomplished fact. The eighth chapter of John's Gospel is a strong example of this. In it Jesus is concentrating everything upon the question of His Person.

"*I am the light of the world . . . The Pharisees therefore said unto him, Thou bearest witness of thyself; thy witness is not true. Jesus answered . . . My witness is true; for I know whence I come, and whither I go; but ye know not whence I come, or whither I go. They said . . . Where is thy Father? Jesus answered . . . Ye know neither me, nor my Father; if ye knew me, ye would know my Father also . . . He said unto them, Ye are from beneath; I am from above: ye are of this world; I am not of this world . . . They said therefore unto him, Who art thou? Jesus said unto them, Even that which*

*I have also spoken unto you from the begin-
ning." (viii, 12-25).*

Then comes the statement which is the turn-
ing point of everything.

"*Jesus therefore said, When ye have lifted
up the Son of man, then ye shall know that I
am he." (viii. 27).*

(But read on to the end of the chapter.)

By something more than implication Jesus had
laid down the same principle with Nicodemus.
Nicodemus was groping in the shadows as to the
Person of Christ. "We know that thou art a
teacher come from God . . ." Jesus pointed out
that, in order to "see," something must take
place by which a new faculty is obtained; a new
birth is necessary. Then He led Nicodemus on
to the Cross, using the same phrase as is in
chapter eight: "As Moses lifted up the serpent
in the wilderness, so must the Son of man be
lifted up" (John iii. 14). The law enunciated
is that it will be the Cross which discloses Who
Jesus is.

Union with God secured for Man in Christ

Within what we have just said lies the
very essence of the significance of Christ.
Let us look briefly at that essential content.
What is *the* thing for which Christ stands pre-

eminently in the whole revelation of Scripture ? The answer is *Union with God.*

That has been the thing for which man has been in quest as long as man has been a sinful creature. In almost countless ways and by as many means he has sought that peace and rest which is to be had alone by oneness with God. Somewhere, somehow (the Bible shows us) a fellowship with God was lost. Three things became the abiding and ever-active marks of this rupture of relationships. One—the lie; two—enmity; and three—death.

The Results of the Fall

(a) A Lie Believed

Man has not only believed and accepted a lie; but it has entered into his constitution, and he is a deceived and darkened soul. Of himself he neither knows, nor is capable of knowing or being, the truth. " *The heart is deceitful above all things, and it is exceedingly corrupt; who can know it?* " (*Jer. xvii.* 9). Man was told that if he took a course contrary to that laid down by God and assumed the right to use his own reason *independently of God* he would be " *as God.*" He accepted the lie, made his bid for supremacy, enthroned his reason in independence, and was taken charge of by the lie. The outworking of this has been—and is—a tremendous development of human achievement by which man has become a lord in his own right (as he thinks) and blinded to the fact that destruction and distress are an ever-growing fruit of his science. So much is this so that the question has been seriously raised by men in a position to ask it, as to whether science is a greater benefactor than it is a curse.

It must be remembered that all unemployment, with its many consequent miseries and troubles, is due to science which has supplanted men by machines, and human skill by mass production. The same responsibility lies at the door of science for the ability to destroy men and the earth on such an immense scale as was unthinkable a generation ago. Project the present course and pace into a few more generations, and what sort of a world will it be ? Of course, the argument is not that science is in itself necessarily evil. There are very many most helpful and valuable discoveries to hand, e.g., chloroform, radium, antiseptics, etc., but our point is that man believes that he is all the time improving, when, as a matter of fact, there is no moral elevation corresponding to the intellectual development.

This matter is not followed out in any measure, but from the simple indication given it can surely be seen that mankind is riding a lie in the form of a tiger which will tear him to pieces*. But

*See note at end of chapter.

the strength of the lie lies in the fact that man does not recognise it, he is blind and in the dark as to its nature and source. This is all the Devil's spite against God.

(b) Enmity Established

The same is true as to the matter of enmity. It is never a far cry from personal interest and self-realisation to war and bloodshed. We do not read of much history between Adam's bid for personal glory and Cain's murder of his brother. The two are one in principle. Whether it be in individual cases, as at the beginning, or in the case of millions locked in deadly destruction of each other, the root is found to be man's desire to acquire. The name Cain means acquisitiveness, or possessiveness. We must be perfectly honest about this. The Christian Church is no exception to this rule. Christians have become divided into thousands of parties, and a very great many of these are antagonistic to each other, or at least distantly suspicious of one another. The enmity amongst believers is taken account of even in the New Testament. It is the Devil's work every time, but even the Devil must have his ground. This he has in the old-creation nature of man. Every division amongst the Lord's people is—in essence—the same as the enmities of the warring Godless world. It is traceable to some old-creation element of *self* asserting itself. There never was —nor will be—a truly Christly division among Christians. Every such division is somewhere a denial and contradiction of Christ. The *apparent* cause may not be some flaming fleshliness, but it will nevertheless be other than the way of Christ. Enmity is a mark of interrupted, arrested, or broken oneness with God; there we leave it for the moment.

(c) Death

The third feature of this destroyed union with God is death. If life is the perfect adjustment and harmony of man with God, then man has not got life. The New Testament assumes this, it does not argue it. Death is not—in the Bible sense—cessation of being, nor is it a state of inanimation. It is just a separation from the source of *true* life, with all the incapacitation which that separation involves. Spiritual death is a powerfully active thing, and in all the things which really relate to God's will it works out in a mighty " cannot."

For the realisation of all God's designs and purposes, and the constituting of the creation which He intends, the possession of His own Divine and uncreated life is essential. Man, by nature, does not possess *that* life, and humanism is one of the most subtle and popular—and the most devastating—forms of the Devil's lie. Hence, man as he is cannot *see* the Kingdom of God. Union with God is a matter of possessing God's life. That provision is an impartation by new birth. Thus we are led up to both the Person and the Cross of Christ.

In Christ a New Humanity

While there yet remain depths too profound and dangerous for even enlightened people of God to attempt to explore, the one thing that is clear as a conclusion is that the Incarnation is intended to set forth the union between God and man, and man and God, which is the Divine intention. Here we have very God joining Himself with very man. But—and let it be well understood—not with *sinful* man, or with our *fallen* humanity. God prepared that body— " that holy thing " (Heb. x. 5; Luke i. 35). When Christ came into this world there came with Him a humanity which—while being *humanity* —was different from all the rest. There were therefore two humanities, one represented uniquely by this solitary Person; the other, by all the rest of men. But even so, His humanity was but a probationary one. Inasmuch as the animating principle of His physical being was blood, He was subject to tiredness, hunger and thirst, and therefore capable of dying and seeing corruption.   That He did die but did *not* see corruption was due to the sovereign intervention of God, and was due to the moral perfection—or holiness—of His nature. " Thou wilt *not* *suffer* thy *Holy One* to see corruption " (Psa. xvi. 10).   The probationary condition of Christ wholly related to His redemptive vocation. When that was accomplished, He still had a human body, but no longer animated by the blood-principle or -basis of life.   Now—while a body —it is a " spiritual body," and therefore a glori-fied body.   It is not unto the likeness of Christ's earthly, pre-resurrection, body that we are to be conformed, but " like unto his glorious body " or " body of glory."*

We are pointing out that in Christ God and man have come together, yet in a Man altogether other than ourselves. This is why union with God —which is the major revelation of the Bible,

---

* I am aware that what has been said above may raise a question as to the " incorruptible blood " of Christ, but my point is in no wise a question as to His moral nature, simply one of His being placed on the basis of life—for the time being—which made it possible for Him to die physically. " Corruption " is only regarded in this sense, not spiritual or moral. I am also aware that physiologists have not yet ended their debate on the seat of corruption, i.e. as to whether it is the blood. But I think that the Bible indicates that it is.

revealed consummately in the New Testament—
is always and *only in Christ.* Until we pass over
on to the resurrection life-basis it will always be
a faith position in Him; not an actual one in our
mortal flesh. But more on this later. In Christ
God has His perfect satisfaction, and has therefore committed Himself to Him. The union is
perfect.

The Lie, Enmity, and Death Annulled in Christ

But this implies or postulates that the three-
fold result and mark of the broken union is absolutely ruled out and non-existent in Christ. Or
to put it round the other way, Christ is the oppo-
site and the negation of the lie, the enmity, and
death. So it is that the most spiritual and
heavenly revelation of Christ, as given in John's
Gospel, is in terms of life, light, and love. Light
and truth are interchangeable names. In this
record Christ makes these things far more than
abstractions, He makes them personal, and says,
' I am these.' There is no darkness, shadow,
lie, or lack of absolute transparency in Him.
There is no enmity, strife, schism, or warfare in
His nature, nor in His attitude or relationship
toward men *as men* (only with evil in the world
and in men) In Him there is no separation from
the Fountain of life. He can say, " I am the

resurrection and the life " (John xi. 25). All this
negation of the results of broken union with God
was because there was no self in Him. It can
be easily seen that the whole effort of the Devil
—in its many forms—was to get Him to act on
some line of self. Self-interest, self-realisation,
self-defence, self-preservation, self-pity, self-
independence, self-resource, etc., etc. To have
succeeded in this matter at any point would have
been to drive a wedge between God and Man
anew, and to have defeated the whole plan of
redemption. But the pure ground of utter self-
lessness was maintained at greatest cost and
through most fiery trial, and the prince of the
world was helpless. The union remained intact.
Life, light, love are triumphant because self is
utterly negatived. But this is all as to Himself,
and thus far it remains His uniqueness. He
abides alone if it stays there.

Christ's Humanity Shared—By the Cross

So we pass on in John's Gospel to the point
at which certain come saying, " We would see
Jesus " (John xii. 21). To this enquiry or quest
Jesus makes a reply which means two things.
One: ' To see me as others are seeing me here
and now is not to see me at all; that is to see
and not perceive.' The other: ' To really see
and know me, union with me in an organic way

is necessary; that is, what is true of me in my relationship with my Father and His relationship with me must become true in an inward way where you are concerned.' Hence: "*Except a grain of wheat fall into the earth and die, it abideth by itself alone; but if it die, it beareth much fruit.*" (*John xii.* 24). 'I did not come to "abide alone." What is true of me as to union with the Father is meant to be for you *in me.*' But at this point we are carried by the Person to the Cross. "*Now is my soul troubled; and what shall I say? Father, save me from this hour. But for this cause came I unto this hour*" (*John xii.* 27). "*And I, if I be lifted up from the earth, will draw all men unto myself. But this he said, signifying by what manner of death he should die*" (*vv.* 32-33).

The Apostle Paul has covered this whole ground in one comprehensive, illuminating, and explanatory statement. We indicate the points of emphasis.

"*The love of Christ constraineth us; because we thus judge, that* one *died for* all, *therefore all died* (*in him*); *and he died for all, that they that live should* no longer live unto themselves, *but* unto him *who for their sakes died and rose again*" (*2 Cor. v.* 14-15).

Someone has freely translated some of the above thus:

"I behold the love of Christ, I see in his

one death the death of all of us already accomplished after the manner of his death—the death of *all that separates us from God.*"

This is all saying very strongly that, to really know Who Christ is as the One in Whom alone God and man are brought together, we must come to the Cross in an experimental way. We must apprehend His death as ours, and then, also in experience—through faith—know a risen life in Him in which the old self-life has been put away.

The Person of Christ Illumined by the Cross

But we must step back for a moment. What was the real meaning of the Cross and what did it effect?   All we have said about the Person of Christ was true of Him altogether apart from the Cross.   For Him the Cross was no necessity.   There came a time, however, when He had to be made what He Himself was not.   To redeem us, He Who knew no sin had to be made sin in our room.   In that hour He was placed in the position of man as the victim of Satan's lie with its darkness.   So also was He made to take upon Him the enmity of our fallen state, and in that deep experience, in that *representative* position He lost the consciousness of the Father's love.   There remained but the third phase of that responsibility—death. For one terrible, eternal 'hour' Christ was separated from —lost union with—His God. "My God, my God, why hast thou forsaken me?" (Matt. xxvii. 46). The mystery is too deep for us, but the fact and the reason are clear and unmistakable.

So He died, "He tasted death"—awful death, which is the full and naked consciousness, awareness, realisation of utter separation from, and abandonment by, God! But in *Himself* He was God's sinless Son, and, as such, He could not be holden of death (Acts ii. 24). In virtue of His essential sinlessness He survived the wrath which rested upon what He was made for that dark hour. He overcame and destroyed the causes, the ground, the strength and the originator of death.

> " By weakness and defeat
>   He won the meed and crown;
> Trod all our foes beneath His feet,
>   By being trodden down.
> He hell in hell laid low,
>   Made sin, He sin o'erthrew;
> Bowed to the grave, destroyed it so,
>   And death by dying slew."

It took more than a man to do this. " *God was in Christ reconciling the world unto Himself* " (2 *Cor. v.* 19).

Thus in the Cross all the cause and nature of separation from God was destroyed, and in Christ risen that union is perfect *for us*. " *There is therefore now no condemnation to them that are in Christ Jesus* " (*Rom. viii.* 1).

This perfect no-condemnation fellowship with God, made actual by the Holy Spirit taking up residence within us through our believing into Christ, is the possession of those alone—but *is* surely the birthright of such—who have come to the Cross in realisation of separation from God, in deepest longing for restored fellowship with Him, and in acknowledgment that sin is the cause. Thus, looking to Christ crucified as the author and perfecter of salvation, they discover that He is more than a man, even man at his greatest. They discover that in Him—and in Him alone—God is found.

Then it works the other way. Can we imagine what Saul of Tarsus felt like — he who had believed Jesus of Nazareth to have been but a man and an impostor among men, and to have been executed as a fraud and blasphemer—when he saw on the Damascus road that this glorified, exalted One was God's eternal Son ? It needed a time in Arabia to let the implications of that adjust and revolutionise his whole outlook.

When we see Whose Cross that was it puts the Cross so far beyond all human ideas of ' dying for ideals, ' ' heroic death for a great cause, ' and all such lesser and altogether inadequate interpretations of Christ's death.

"Ye killed the Prince of life" (Acts iii. 15) was the charge laid at the Jews' door by the Apostles.

So we come back to our starting point. It requires the Cross to really see Who Jesus is; and in the seeing of Him truly by the Cross we see how great, wonderful, sacred, and awful is that Cross.

No wonder that Satan has ever sought to take from His essential Person and make Him something less! No wonder that he has so persistently sought to strip the Cross of its truest meaning! Let all who do either of these things recognise from whence their inspiration, or blindness, comes, and with whom it is that they—though unintentionally—are in league.

Let Christians also realise that all enmity; lack of love, divisions, and strife; all prejudice, suspicion, and spiritual blindness; with all spiritual death, is because the Cross has not been apprehended aright. Somewhere uncrucified flesh is holding the ground. It is impossible to be a truly crucified man or woman and at the same time either have personal interests or be at variance with other children of God, i.e. without love for them. The essential basis of life, light, and love—which is Christ in full manifestation—is the Cross as a working reality in the realm of the old creation, and the risen power of Christ in the new.

All this is but saying in other words that the Cross of Christ brings us into living union and oneness with God, and if we will but live in the full meaning and value of that union we shall be living epistles of Christ in terms of life, light, and love. Failure in these means failure somewhere, and for some reason, in our fellowship with God in Christ. The measure of our walk with Him will be the measure of these three features of Christ.

Notes from the recent writings of a Scientist.

" The clever craftsman has gradually become displaced; his successor is a machine oiler and switch attendant . . . "

" Science is constantly boasting of the benefits it is conferring on the poor; why then the world-wide impoverishment, hunger and mal-nutrition, and almost universal discontent? Why does science produce year by year huge gluts of food that are never consumed, when prices are so heavily loaded against the consumer? Is it not wanton for science to stand idly looking on when twenty-seven million bags of coffee are burnt in Brazil, when millions of acres of cotton are ploughed up, when millions of young pigs are slaughtered, when hundreds of millions of unsold herrings are thrown back into the sea?"

" We are seriously told to picture a bomb which will blow the British Isles half-way across the Atlantic."

" Science has become the arch-enemy of the Christian faith."

" All down the ages warriors have constantly sought new and more effective weapons with which to butcher the other side. In the eighteenth century the French schools of gunnery were the only places where science was systematically taught. Science was then rarely more than a responsive handmaid to the ever clamant demands of war."

" Both history and science give us warrant for believing that humanity has made great advances in accumulating knowledge and experience and in devising instruments of living, and the value of all these is indisputable. But they do not constitute real progress in human nature itself, and in the absence of such progress those gains are external, precarious, and *liable to be turned to our own destruction* " (italics ours).

(Surely this—a mere fragment of a whole volume—bears out the words of the Apostle: " And so the word of the Scripture comes true: ' I will destroy the wisdom of the wise, I will make nothing of the intelligence of those who profess to know.' . . . God makes the wisdom of the world foolishness, for as it was in that wisdom that the world lost the knowledge of God, it was by reason of that that its eyes were closed, and lo! the wisdom of God now appearing is proclaimed as a foolish thing, foolish in the sight of that old wisdom. It does not commend itself to the old wisdom . . . Christ is the wisdom of God, and the power of God. There is more wisdom in God's ' foolishness ' than in men's cleverness " [I Cor. i. 18—25].)

CHAPTER II.

The Cross and the Holy Spirit

" And Jesus, when he was baptized, went up straightway from the water: and lo, the heavens were opened unto him, and he saw the Spirit of God descending as a dove, and coming upon him "—(Matt. iii. 16).

" Christ redeemed us from the curse of the law, having become a curse for us; for it is written, Cursed is every one that hangeth on a tree: that upon the Gentiles might come the blessing of Abraham in Christ Jesus; that we might receive the promise of the Spirit through faith."—(Gal. iii. 13-14).

The matter to which we are directed now is the Cross and the Holy Spirit. Let me say at the outset that this is not a treatise on the Person and work of the Holy Spirit, but primarily an emphasis upon the relationship between the Holy Spirit and the Cross of Christ.

God Working by His Spirit

Before we can come immediately to that matter, there are some preliminary things that

31

it will be helpful to remember. They are of a more general character. Firstly there is this fact, that the Scriptures make it quite clear that whenever God has moved to realize any phase of His comprehensive purpose, He has done so bv the agency of His Spirit. The Spirit of God has been the wisdom, the power, the energy, the initiator, the continuer and the consummator of that which God has at any time taken in hand to bring about. That is quite patent to all, I think, on the most superficial glance at the Scriptures.

We see it in creation, that is, the creation of this world. The Spirit of God is there as the agent initiating, pervading, conducting and always in evidence in relation to the bringing of this cosmic order into being.

The same is seen to be true in the history and life of Israel. The whole of their life and the ordering of their life was a matter of the Spirit of God. He worked with their fathers, He led them out of Egypt as the pillar of fire and cloud, He sustained them in the wilderness; He endowed men amongst them for the framing, the making, the constituting of that great symbolism of Christ—the tabernacle. Bezalel and Oholiab were men peculiarly endowed by the Spirit of God unto all manner of work in connection with the tabernacle, and in many other ways and connections it is seen that the Spirit of the Lord was in charge of this whole matter of Israel's life and history. God was fulfilling His purpose, or that phase of His great purpose, by the agency of His Spirit.

What was true in those connections is seen to be true in the case of the life and work of the Lord Jesus; begotten of the Holy Ghost, anointed of the Spirit, fulfilling His ministry, uttering His teaching, performing His works, all by that anointing of the Spirit, and eventually offering Himself to God without spot " through the eternal Spirit." In *all* things, again, God carries out His work by means of His Spirit.

And then we pass on to the Church. It becomes abundantly clear that this great aspect of the purpose of God through the ages is again in the hands of the Holy Spirit. The Church is brought into being by the Holy Spirit on the day of Pentecost, and from that time everything is committed to the Spirit to carry out.

What is true as to the Church, its calling, its vocation, its purpose, is true, according to the Scriptures, of every member thereof, every individual. The life of every child of God is begun by the Holy Spirit, born of the Spirit; and then to be, under the Spirit's conducting, led into all the will and thoughts and ways of the Lord; perfected by the Spirit; saved, sanctified and glorified, all by the Spirit of God.

That is a very elementary consideration, I know, but it is basic because the assumption is this, that man has in himself none of the requirements, moral, intellectual or spiritual, for realizing any part of God's purpose. If it were possible for man to do so, then the Spirit of God need not have come ; but the very coming of the Spirit is the great Divine declaration that God must do His own work or it will never be done—that man is totally incapable of realizing any part or fragment of the great purpose of God, and, without the Spirit, no part thereof will ever be realized. That is what it means that the Spirit of God is always in charge of the things of God, because man is not capable in that realm.

So the advent of the Holy Spirit is nothing less than the very advent of God Himself to project, to constitute and to accomplish a new spiritual creation, a spiritual cosmos (I very much dislike that word, but it is a fuller word than ' world ' and it means something more than even a creation, it is an ordered system)—the advent of God the Holy Spirit is to project and constitute and consummate a new ordered spiritual system, a spiritual cosmos, an entirely spiritual nature of things of which the natural and the physical is but a shadow, a type.

Christ a Comprehensive Spiritual System

Now, the pattern of this spiritual order or system or economy is God's own Son, Jesus

Christ.   Christ is a vast and comprehensive spiritual system and order.   That does not mean that He is not a person, an individual, but He is something more than that.   In His Person there is the embodiment of this vast, this comprehensive, system of Divine thoughts, of Divine elements, of Divine laws, Divine principles and Divine nature.   This physical universe we know, and are learning more and more, to be a vast system of laws and principles. It is a great whole, inter-related, inter-dependent, moving together by influences and forces and tides, bound up as a marvellous order and harmony, nothing just taking its own independent course, nothing unrelated, nothing unaffected by the rest ; one marvellous whole. And the knowledge of this physical universe is more than a matter of a life's application, a lifetime's study.   It has taken all the generations from the beginning to reach even the present point which those who know most admit to be far short of all that we have yet to know about this universe.   When you read some of the works of men who know what there is to be known now, your very brain reels when you read of distances and speeds in this universe, the rate at which light travels, and all these things ; I say it is a vast order, and it is more than a lifetime's study for understanding.

But, my dear friends, we have said that the

physical universe is only a symbol, a type, of the spiritual, and Christ is a universe, a universe of spiritual laws, of spiritual principles, of spiritual forces. Christ is a vast unity, a marvellous harmony, and when you begin to glimpse that, you just begin to understand what the Apostles have seen or begun to see when they themselves are found in the grip of a passionate quest to know Him. " *That I may know him* " (*Phil. iii.* 10). " *I count all things to be loss for the excellency of the knowledge of Christ Jesus my Lord* " (*Phil. iii.* 8). This even at the end of a lifetime of learning Christ, this even after marvellous revelations in heaven itself of things unspeakable which it is not lawful for a man to utter ; still in the grip of this tremendous quest—" that I may know Him."

Then you understand also why there is coming from that this urge, this constant and ever increasing urge upon believers to follow on to know the Lord, to go on to know. You understand the meaning of a little prefix which is, I think, tremendously impressive. They not only speak about knowledge, the knowledge of Christ, the knowledge of God, the knowledge of the Lord ; not only do they so often use that word ' gnosis,' but you find later, as they have moved on, they introduce this combination ' epignosis.' " Till we all attain unto . . . the *full*-knowledge . ." (*Eph.* iv. 13); not merely " the knowledge " now. This is to Ephesians, those well on in knowledge. (If you care to look up the usage of that particular form of the word you will find it tremendously impressive, as it is seeking to take believers beyond even a fairly matured stage of spiritual life.) Here, then, is their own quest ; here is their urge upon the saints, because they have glimpsed by revelation of the Holy Spirit something of this vast comprehensiveness of Christ. He is a universe, a new and entirely different system of things spiritually. Who knows anything about it? What do we know about Christ? We may have been the Lord's people for a good many years. The fact is that the longer we live and the more we are associated and in touch with things of Christ the more we are overwhelmed with our ignorance, because we are realizing that Christ is a land of far distances. He is so far beyond us, we cannot comprehend Him. "Brethren, I count not myself to have apprehended" (Phil. iii. 13). That is Paul near the end of his course. "I press on," "that I may know him." Yes, Christ is a universe of Divine thoughts, Divine laws, Divine principles, all of the most practical character, and I do want to underline that statement, because what I am saying may be regarded as something very abstract.

But come back to the analogy, to the type. Are these things in the physical universe abstract ? Are they without practical meaning and value ? We know that these forces and these laws at work are the very things which make life possible upon this earth. What would happen but for the effect of the heavenly bodies upon this earth ? The very tides of the sea are governed by heavenly bodies. Every time the tide rises on our shores, it is in response to a great governing body in the heavens. Every time the tide recedes and goes out, it is simply obeying a heavenly power; and the tides are of value, they do mean something. And in many other connections it is like that. Our life here on this earth is only possible because of this ordered universe and the influences at work as from without ; and in this universe of Christ our very life, our very coming to the great goal for which we are destined by God, depends upon our response to the laws of Christ, our reaction to the influences of Christ, and upon our knowledge of these things—because in this realm it is God's will that we should understand these things, we should have understanding in Christ, we should be intelligent. So far as this physical universe is concerned, in order to derive the benefits we do not all have to be scientists. We are getting benefits every day without understanding any of these things ; but in the spiritual realm it is God's thought that we should know.

Seeing the Greatness of Christ
by the Holy Spirit

All this brings us to the whole matter of the Holy Spirit. What do we know of Christ after all? If we know Him as our Saviour, our Redeemer, our Lord, our High Priest, our Advocate on high, in all these ways, what do we know of Him after all? That is nothing. Paul knew all that, but here he is speaking and acting as one who knew nothing, because the knowledge yet to be possessed was so far beyond anything already attained unto. We know nothing.

But the advent of the Spirit, the coming of the Spirit, has had that whole matter in view —to lead us into this vast universe which Christ is, this wonderful spiritual system and order of things of which Christ is the embodiment, to make us know in continual progress and development more of the meaning of Christ. I know I am failing to convey to you the tremendous impression that this has made on my own heart as I have thought about it, as it has come to me. As I stand so far behind these Apostles but listen to what they say, the impression to begin with is that these men have evidently seen something in Christ that is immense and it has taken out of their lives anything in the nature of spiritual contentedness with their apprehension, with their attainment. This that they have glimpsed has made them men who are on full stretch to know all that it is possible to know, not because they are just men of an inquisitive turn of mind who want to know for the sake of knowledge, but they see that that knowledge is unto the fulness of God's purpose in their own lives and in their lives as related to a Body, the Body of Christ, His Church. The Church will never go on to that realization, and the individual members of the Church will never grow, save as the Church and the members thereof glimpse something of the greatness of Christ. The way of spiritual growth is the glimpsing of the greatness of Christ by revelation of the Holy Spirit, and that is why Paul prayed as he did " *having the eyes of your heart enlightened, that ye may know what is the hope of his calling, what the riches of the glory of his inheritance in the saints, and what the exceeding greatness of his power to us-ward who believe* " (*Eph. i.* 18-19); that you might know this by His giving to you " *a spirit of wisdom and revelation in the 'epignosis' (in the full knowledge) of him.*" That is how the Church will grow, that is how the saints will make increase—seeing in a new way how vast and great is Christ.

Do you not agree that among all the needs

that exist to-day in the people of God one of the most potent is the need to be delivered from spiritual contentedness, satisfaction with a small measure of the Christian life ? There is a sad, a tragic absence of a really adequate reach out to know Him. Oh, I know that needs perhaps qualifying and covering. There are many people who say they want to know and want to go on, but their quest, their desire, is not of that character, that nature, which obtained in the case of the Apostle Paul—" I count all things but loss for the excellency of the knowledge of Christ Jesus my Lord." All *things*.

With many Christians and Christian workers, if you touch their work, their organization, their system of things, their religious thing of which they are part, then you meet awful resistance, Prejudices and suspicions and all those things rise out of this weddedness to things rather than to the Lord. If only people were wedded to the Lord and He was their only quest, you would get rid of 95 per cent of all the prejudice and suspicion that exists. It is things that produce it. We need to drop our things and be found only concerned with the Lord. Our one question, governing every situation, should be, Does that contribute in any way to a larger measure of Christ ? If it does, then in my heart I am with it; it does not matter what it does to existing institutions. If that can lead on to a knowledge of Christ beyond what we have, then that is the thing that matters. It is Christ, not *our* Church, not *our* fellowship, not *our* mission, not *our* organization, not *our* tradition, but Christ. He is a tremendously enlarging and emancipating factor. It is these things that have cramped us down and made us small, mean, petty and peevish. Christ delivers, Christ enlarges ; oh, to see Him ! Oh, that we could be brought by the Spirit as the Queen of Sheba was brought and shown the kingdom of Solomon, his glory, his table, his servants, until there was no more spirit left in her and she said, " *I heard . . . of thine acts and thy wisdom. Howbeit I believed not . . . until I came and mine eyes had seen it: and behold, the half was not told me* " (1 *Kings x.* 7). And a greater than Solomon is here ! What you and I need is that enlargement which comes by a Holy Spirit inward revelation of Christ and we shall be emancipated. These other things will fall into their own place as we see Him more fully.

That, then, is the very meaning of the Holy Spirit having come. I say again, what do we know ? How small is our knowledge ! Ah, but God knows that, and the Spirit of God has come. What for ? To be at our service, for us to use, that He might be taken hold of to give us prominence and importance and name and reputation ? No, He has come for no other purpose than to bring God's Son into ever-increasing fulness in the saints, to make Christ in the Church what He is in the sight of God, that He may become in the Church the " fulness of him that filleth all in all." That is the Holy Spirit's purpose in coming. Well, what a heritage we have when we have the Holy Spirit !—" the Spirit which is an *earnest* of our inheritance " (Eph. i. 14). With the Holy Spirit, all the inheritance is bound up and guaranteed. Having the Spirit, all that fulness is potentially ours.

Now it is for us to be taught by the Spirit, and the Holy Spirit does not teach us as out of a book, as by a manual. He does not teach us just by addresses and talks and lectures, not by words as such. The Holy Spirit teaches by practical experience, and the instrument of the Holy Spirit's teaching of Christ is the Cross of Christ. You and I will learn nothing except as the Holy Spirit makes the Cross of Christ a reality in us. We shall come to that presently.

The Unity of Christ

I am first of all concerned with this emphasis upon the greatness of Christ, the vastness of Christ, and the fact that the Holy Spirit has come to bring that greatness into the Church. There is so much detail bound up with that. We have referred to the laws and relationships and dependencies and inter-dependencies of this physical universe. Christ is that; difficult as it is for us to grasp, Christ is that. And then the Church has to be the reproduction of what Christ is, so that in the Body of Christ you find all these spiritual laws of inter-relatedness, inter-dependence, and no member of the Body can say to any other member, however remote the other member may be in the matter of distance and position, " I have no need of thee " (1 Cor. xii. 21). The head cannot say to the feet —there are your extremities!—' Because you are so far removed from me, I am not dependent upon you.' It cannot be. " The eye cannot say to the hand, I have no need of thee." Proximity makes no difference in this matter, distance makes no difference. The relatedness constitutes the Body a perfect whole, a perfect *one*, a perfect harmony, all inter-dependent, inter-related. That is Christ. " So also is the Christ " (1 Cor. xii. 12 Gr.).

And in the realm of the Spirit that sort of thing is going on. We need, of course, spiritual perception to be able to grasp it. It may be that a very great deal of our spiritual experience which cannot be explained at all by anything within the immediate circle of our lives is due to something that is going on in some children of God or child of God far removed from us geographically. There may be some tremendous conflict in a life, or in a company of the Lord's people, on the other side of the world, and because the Spirit is one we are involved in that conflict, and we are going through something, and we are moved to pray, and the issue is one issue. Geography does not touch it. Very often we do not understand what is the meaning of that through which we are passing. We know of certain things in our spiritual experience, something is going on, there is conflict on, there is pressure on, and there is nothing immediately around us to explain it. There is no occasion for it so far as we can see here and now. But there is some issue in the balances, some issue over which there is spiritual conflict somewhere, and because the Spirit is one and the Body is one, we are bound up with that conflict. That is the oneness, the harmony of Christ, that is the interaction of these laws of one Body, a new spiritual system. Some of us have known how true these things are and how very practical they are. If the Church only had intelligence about this and lived up to its intelligence, what loss it would be to the enemy! How often the children of God are caught misinterpreting their experience, things that are happening, what is going on in another life. The enemy puts a false construction upon a thing, and, instead of bringing those concerned together to co-operate for victory, he sets them apart by mis-construction. If the Church saw this spiritual oneness, this spiritual inter-relatedness, inter-dependence, and threw itself right into that, what a mighty thing the Church would be here in this universe! And that is the spiritual system that Christ is, which is to be constituted in His Body, reproduced in His Church.

You say that it is a hopeless thing to expect so far as the whole Church is concerned. It is a very beautiful ideal, but what are the prospects of realization? Well, we cannot dismiss it like that. We have to come back. It will begin, perhaps, between two of us, and that will constitute a sufficient ground for instruction and for victory, for understanding. Even the perfect harmony of two children of God is a terrific cause of battle, but get it and see what an effective thing it is for God! And that is why the battle rages—just to separate two children of God who are vitally related. Satan has always tried that, and what things come in to do it!

The Cross Basic to all the Spirit's Work

That brings us to that to which we have been working, the Cross and the Holy Spirit; for the basis and the door of all the Spirit's work is the Cross. You will, with the slightest knowledge of the Old and New Testament Scriptures, at once recall very much that brings these two together. Back in the types we see them brought together; in the fire upon the altar—the altar typifying the Cross, and the fire upon the altar the Spirit consuming the sacrifice. Or again, as in Ex. xvii, the rock smitten and the gushing water—the Cross and the Spirit. Or, coming to the New Testament, the Jordan of our Lord's baptism setting forth in type His death and burial and resurrection, immediately issuing in the open heavens and the Spirit in dove-like form resting upon Him—the Cross and the Spirit. Or, going back with that in mind to Israel's beginnings as a nation, the lamb slain, the blood sprinkled, the pillar of cloud and fire taking charge immediately afterwards—the Spirit by way of the Cross ; all pointing to the great inclusive reality, Calvary and Pentecost. It is always like that. The two are always together. And these are but fragmentary selections of a vast amount in the Word of God which shows this close and inseparable oneness between the two.

When we come to the Lord Jesus, we know that His very messages or discourses on the Holy Spirit in a definite and specific way were reserved until the eve of the passion. It was with the shadow of the Cross thrown fully across His path that He began to speak about the coming of the Comforter and what that coming would mean to them ; and He never did say, "Receive ye the Holy Spirit" (John xx. 22) until He could show them His hands and His side, His pierced hands, His riven side. Just as the Spirit came on Him at the time of His typical death in baptism, so that Spirit led Him to the actual Cross, where we are told He "through the eternal Spirit offered himself without blemish unto God" (Heb. ix. 14). Well, if it were necessary, much more could be gathered to show how the two are kept together —the Cross and the Spirit. The Cross leads to the Spirit and the Spirit ever brings back to the Cross.

Why is the Cross basic to the Spirit's work ? Our passage in Gal. iii. gives the answer. Because a curse exists, is resting now upon the old creation, "Christ redeemed us from the curse of the law, having become a curse for us," or, literally and correctly, "having become a curse in our place." The human race by nature lies under a curse and the Holy Spirit can never, never, come upon an accursed thing. The promise of the Spirit can never be fulfilled in those who still remain under the curse. The curse must be removed, for the anointing oil shall come upon no flesh; "upon the flesh of man shall it not be poured" (Ex. xxx. 32). The curse must be removed, and Christ redeemed us from the curse of the law, having become a curse in our stead, in order that we might receive the promise of the Spirit. The removing of a whole condition and state under a curse in order to clear the way for the Spirit—that is the answer. Therein lies the necessity for the Cross and for our faith identification with Him Who was made a curse for us. And, however uncomfortable and unlovely it may sound, the fact is that when the Holy Spirit really gets to work in a life, on the one side the course and history for that life is such as to make the one concerned very well aware that the flesh is an accursed thing.

There are no people in this world who are more ready to admit and acknowledge the accursed nature of the flesh than those who have the Spirit. It is the very pathway to glory to discover how accursed the flesh is. That is on one side. No doubt many of us know something of that history. The Holy Spirit really does make the meaning of the Cross known in that sense that the Cross speaks of a place where a curse is, and we are there in Christ. Something in the way has got to be removed.

Here, in the case of these Galatians, the Apostle says that they had begun in the Spirit; did they hope to be perfected in the flesh ? And bringing in this passage, it makes the question very emphatic and very terrible. Having begun in the Spirit—which pre-supposes that you are outside of the curse to be able to make a beginning at all, to have any prospect of going on—do you think you are going to be perfected by getting back under the curse ? No; the argument is that that is only to close the door again, to cut off all the prospect, to bar the way to any further progress. "Having begun in the Spirit, are ye now perfected in the flesh ? " The deduction, while not exactly stated, but quite clearly implied, is that, having begun in the Spirit it is only possible to continue in the Spirit on the ground on which you made a beginning. That is, by the Cross you get away and continually keep away from that ground of the curse; or, in other words, your progress requires the continual position to which the Cross brings you, just as your beginning required that position. That is, to continue is to continue in the Spirit.

But you can continue in the Spirit only as you began in the Spirit. That was only made possible by the Cross removing the curse, the old man, the accursed old man. So that to continue in the Spirit, to go right on to all that the Spirit intends, means, and is after, demands a continual cutting off of the flesh, a keeping cut off of the flesh by the Cross. So the Spirit keeps the Cross in evidence, and the Cross makes all the Spirit's purpose possible.

We have not to be continually occupied with our crucifixion; the Holy Spirit will attend to that. We have to walk in the Spirit. To do this we have just to obey the Spirit. It is positive, not negative.

In the New Testament letters we get a many-sided application of the Cross as the Spirit's instrument. Let us look at some of these. Firstly there is " Romans " which has to do with

The Cross and the Sinful Body of the Flesh

Up to chapter vii. everything circles round and centres in the Cross. The Cross is the great issue toward which everything is intended to lead. The Apostle steadily and thoroughly works his way to that climax. All that is in those seven chapters finds its end in the position set forth in the words of chapter vi. 3-11, and especially in verses 3, 5, 6: "*. . . all we who were baptized into Christ Jesus were baptized into his death . . . we have become united with Him in the likeness of his death . . . our old man was crucified with him, that the body of sin might be done away.*" Until this has become a position established and entered into, the revelation of a life in the Spirit is not touched upon. But when this has become basic, then we have all that follows about the Spirit's presence and work.

"*Ye are . . . in the Spirit, if . . . the Spirit of God dwelleth in you. But if any man hath not the Spirit of Christ, he is none of his* " (viii. 9).

" The law of the Spirit of life in Christ Jesus made me free from the law of sin and death " (*viii.* 2).

" The mind of the spirit is life and peace " (*viii.* 6).

And so on.

Here, then, the specific emphasis is upon the fact that, for the presence and work of the Holy Spirit in the believer and the " Body " (chapter xii.) to be really known, the whole body of sin (the man out of Christ being a sinful creature and lying under judgment and condemnation) must be—not reformed, remedied, improved, educated to better things—but crucified and buried; not just sins being taken away or pardoned, but *himself* put away. As a man he must depart from God's sight, his good (?) and his bad. He belongs by nature to a race which no longer stands in the light of God's intention. God has departed from that race, and has made a " new creation." Christ in resurrection is the " firstborn among many brethren." He is " the last Adam," meaning that as the first of a new race, a new humanity, finality is with Him; there will be no need of another. This " last Adam " stepped back—so to speak—and before becoming in resurrection the " firstborn from the dead," He gathered up all the race of the first Adam and representatively took it into the full judgment of God-forsakenness, crying " My God, my God, why hast thou forsaken me ? " That is God's ultimate mind toward the whole race in the first Adam. We are called upon to recognize that, to take a position and make a declaration that we accept Christ's death as our death and His burial as our burial. The New Testament says that that is the declaration which baptism makes, or that that declaration is made in baptism.

While very much more ought to be said on this whole matter, we will gather it up in this inclusive observation, that the position in " Romans " is God's foundation, and it is all-comprehensive. A Holy Spirit-governed life will be brought back to the implications of the Cross as the end of the old man. There will be one basic crisis, but through the years there may be many crises in which we have to refer back to the orginal inclusive position fresh issues which have been raised as we could bear to know them. The final position which the Cross establishes and to which the Holy Spirit works is that all shall be—in every direction and con-nection—Christ only, and not ourselves in any respect. Thus we are led to the next specific application of the Cross as in the First Letter to the Corinthians.

The Cross and the Natural Man

Here those concerned are in Christ. So far

as the " Romans " situation is concerned as to
" justified in Christ," the position is all right.
Their standing is complete; they have accepted
Christ as their substitute. It is not that they are
in the flesh, but that the flesh is in them, and
they are being largely influenced and actuated
by natural considerations. In their case it is
the natural or soulical man who is riding over
the spiritual man. " Natural " in 1 Corinthians
is, in the Greek, " soulical." The Apostle
explains what " soulical " means when he points
out that their own minds and hearts and wills
are governing instead of the mind of Christ by
the Holy Spirit. Their reasonings, judgments,
ideas, standards of values—" the wisdom of the
world "—result in their unspiritual and un-
Christlike behaviour. The soul-life finds its way
even into the most spiritual realms; e.g. spiritual
gifts, to use them for self-glory; the Lord's Table,
to turn it to self-gratification; etc. Thus their
progress toward the full purpose of being " In
Christ " is retarded; they are not spiritual but
" carnal "; not grown up ones but " babes."

In this connèction the Apostle says: " I determined not to know anything among you, save
Jesus Christ and him crucified " (1 Cor. ii. 2).
What is needed is that application of the Cross,
not to make us saved men and women in a
general sense, but to deliver us from our own
souls as they overflow the life of the Spirit in

us. The Cross must clear the way for the Spirit, and what must be dealt with is the dominance of our own soul-life.

We pass to another phase of the Cross and the Holy Spirit when we come to the Letter to the Galatians. Here it is:

The Cross and Legalism

You will remember how much there is in this letter concerning the Spirit and the Cross. Look at the following two series of passages—(a) Chapter iii. 2, 3, 5, 14; iv. 6; v. 5, 16, 17, 18, 22, 25; vi. 8. (b) ii. 20; iii. 1; v. 24; vi. 14.

What then is the point in this combination of the two—the Cross and the Spirit? The Galatians were being urged and tempted to return to the old legal order of " Thou shalt " and " Thou shalt not "; to the outward imposition of the whole system of religious regulations and rules; to the strait-jacket of legalism. Legalism is not only Jewish, it is a persistent tendency. It is the easiest thing into which to fall. It is so easy for a person who has the Spirit to begin to lay down the law to others; to say, ' You ought (or, ought not) to do this or that '; or, ' You must give up (or adopt) this or that.' Thus the strait-jacket of legal bondage is imposed, and it is forgotten that the main need is not law but that the Spirit should be Lord within, and that when this is so, many things will fall off, and those concerned will know what the Lord requires of them. This, as the Apostle says in this letter, is the way of sonship and liberty. The Lord within can be trusted, and hands need not be put upon lives to govern them. Let it be said quite definitely here that, as it was circumcision particularly which occasioned this letter to the Galatians, so it may be (and often is) some one or more of the Christian ordinances or forms or orders or observances which are made focal points of legal pressure and crisic issues. Important as such things may be, we cannot be too strong in pointing out that they may safely be subjected to what is supremely important, that is to say, if the Cross has really been so truly wrought in a life as to deliver from bondage to tradition, popular acceptances, and indeed all that is but the letter apart from the Spirit, thus giving a full and clear way for the absolute sovereignty of the Holy Spirit within the life, all such things will take care of themselves, and they will be brought in (that is, those which are required by the Lord) in a *living*, rather than a legal and dead way. But what a mighty work it is for the Cross to have delivered from the inheritance of generations! Setness and finality are features of a legal system, and make spiritual growth and enlargement impossible. Truth without life is fatal, as is righteousness without love. Prejudice and suspicion are fruits of bondage to some religious *thing* and not of the Spirit.

It is possible to have the most perfect New Testament order and framework, and a most devoted adherence to the letter of the Word, but to be almost totally devoid of life and unction. This is usually due to a failure in a deep experimental working of the Cross and the consequent hindering of the Spirit.

Every one of these aspects of the Cross and the Holy Spirit ought to have a volume to itself, and we are only able to give here the vital points. We shall now pass on to those companion letters known to us as " Ephesians " and " Colossians," but more truly, circular letters to churches in an area. Here the particular application relates to:

Deliverance from the Earthlies

and the matter in view is THE FULNESS OF CHRIST. In " Colossians " it is fulness in Christ as Head of the Church, the Body. " *He is the head of the body, the church: . . . that in him should all the fulness dwell* " (*i.* 18, 19). " *. . . in whom are all the treasures of wisdom and knowledge . . .* " (*ii.* 3). " *In him dwelleth all the fulness . . . and in him ye are made full* " (*ii.* 9, 10), etc.

In " Ephesians," the fulness is in Christ *in*

the Church. " . . . *gave him to be head over all things to the church, which is his body, the fulness of him that filleth all in all* " (*i.* 22, 23). "*. . . that ye may be filled unto all the fulness of God* " (*iii.* 19). "*. . . till we all attain unto . . . the fulness of Christ* " (*iv.* 13).

This is all revealed to be the object of " the eternal purpose," the "counsel of his will." It dates back to before times eternal and on to " the ages of the ages." It is a vast and unspeakable Divine intention, and one unto which not all will attain. It costs the Apostle much travail, agony, and striving on behalf of the Church (Col. i. 28—ii. 1).

This " attaining " demands a special application of the Cross and consequent operation of the Holy Spirit. A phrase particularly characteristic of these letters is "the heavenlies." " Ephesians " has it five times, and the point is carried on in " Colossians " (see Eph. i. 3, 20; ii. 6; iii. 10; vi. 12; Col. iii. 1, 2). This is shown to mean a spiritual position, life, and vocation, and when we look at the context we find that it is of very practical implications. Of course, it is especially related to the Church, the Body, and is corporate; but what is true of the Body must be true of every member, hence many personal exhortations. The practical implications referred to combine to emphasize that " fulness " is heavenly and spiritual, and therefore the Lord's people

—if they are to attain, not to salvation but to
" purpose "—must live on the heavenly line.
Thus, all merely earthly features as governing
factors have to be left behind. There is nationality. " There cannot be Greek and Jew." We
have got to leave that ground, both as to ourselves and others. If we stand on national
ground, which not only means nationalism, but
temperament and disposition, we are going to
cut short spiritual growth. The same applies
to the social—" bondman, freeman "; to race or
civilization—" barbarian, Scythian "; to religious rites—" circumcision, uncircumcision " (Col.
iii. 10-11).

The point is this: Christ is in heaven. He is
there as " head of the body." Christ is essentially a heavenly Man, representative of a new
humanity, not of this divided, conflicting, chaotic,
disrupted race. He is other and different.
Divine fulness will be only known in Him *as
such*. We have got to leave the ground of this
humanity at every point and *live on the ground
of Christ*—where " Christ is all and in all."

To do otherwise is to lower Christ, to divide
Christ, and to limit Christ.

Unto this heavenly position and fulness the
Holy Spirit has come to lead the Church—which,
as the " One Body," cannot recognize or tolerate
schism or divisions except to its own destruction.
So we have in these companion letters much

about the Holy Spirit. See Eph. i. 3 (instead of "spiritual blessing" it should be "blessing of the Spirit") i. 13, 14, 17; ii. 18, 22; iii. 5, 16; iv. 3, 4, 30; v. 9, 18; vi. 17, 18; Col. i. 8.

But this work of the Spirit demands that the Cross has really come in between earth and heaven, and that—because of it—in a true spiritual apprehension we have taken our place with Christ in heaven. "*Made us to sit with him in the heavenlies in Christ Jesus.*"

Because of the advanced position set forth, the Cross is largely taken for granted in "Ephesians."

"*We have our redemption through his blood, the forgiveness of our trespasses.*" "*The exceeding greatness of his power to usward who believe . . . which he wrought in Christ, when he raised him from the dead . . .*" "*And you did he quicken when you were dead . . . and raised us up with him.*" "*That ye put away . . . the old man . . . and put on the new man.*" (*Eph.* i. 7, 19; ii. 1, 6; iv. 22, 24).

In Colossians it is more definite still. (See ii. 11, 12, 13, 20; iii. 3, 9).

It is a vast revelation which is given in these letters, a "land of far distances" and of inexhaustible riches. We shall only keep ourselves out of it if we live on, and become actuated by, earthly considerations. Here we are forbidden to talk in a discriminating way, either favourably or unfavourably, about British, American, Chinese, German, etc.; social distinctions; or any other feature of the old humanity. If that were our realm of business and sole considera- tion then we should have to be so affected; but in Christ's interests and in the Church we are crucified to all this, and now we seek to meet believers solely on the ground of Christ. Only so can there be the building up of the Body. There are many other dividing factors among the Lord's people, both as to their natural con- stitution and their religious acceptance. The Cross is the remedy for all, and the Spirit of God demands the Cross if spiritual fulness is to be reached.

Our final word for the present will arise from the Letter to the Philippians. It is the climax of the risen life.

The Cross and the Throne

In the first place the case of Christ is cited as an example. "*Existing in God-form . . . emptied himself, taking the form of a bond- servant . . . humbled himself, becoming obedient unto death, yea, the death of the cross. Where- fore also God highly exalted him, and gave unto him the name which is above every name . . .*" (*ii.* 5-9).

Then the Apostle is seen to be aspiring with

a tremendous aspiration unto something that he calls " the prize of the on-high calling " (iii. 14). It looks very much as though this is all of a piece with the call and promise to the Over-comers of the Laodicean Church. " He that overcometh, I will give to him to sit down with me in my throne . . ." (Rev. iii. 21).

Thus it is clear from these Scriptures that (1) not all will " attain," and (2) a special work of the Cross is basic to attaining. The Cross has to deal with our ' mindedness.' " Have this mind in you." " Emptied himself." This ' mindedness ' is seen in Paul. " I count all things to be loss . . . and do count them but refuse." Into the balances with the throne both Christ and Paul placed all *personal* " gain." Position, rights, reputation, advantages, etc.; this was the way and outworking of the Cross. " Obedient unto death." " Becoming conformed unto his death."

It is all so much a matter of ' mindedness.' There was a situation at Philippi which repre-sented a real hindrance to that " pressing on " and " attaining," a real menace and threat to the " prize "; a real challenge to " the on-high calling." Two people were not of one mind; there was a clash and a breach. The implica-tions seem to be that personal interests and earthly considerations were the strength of this strain. Only as the Cross dealt with *that*

' mindedness,' and made way for Christ-minded-
ness could the way be cleared for apprehending
that for which they had been apprehended by
Christ Jesus.   Satan is terribly against saints
coming to the throne.   That throne and that
transcendent Name mean his final undoing.   He
knows that a ' mindedness ' which is not the
fruit of death to self and resurrection to Christ
alone can frustrate that Divine " calling." Everything, then, lies behind this throne-union—
" Romans,"   " Corinthians,"   " Galatians,"
" Ephesians," " Colossians," and " Philippians,"
in their specific and cumulative application of
the truth that the Spirit always works by the
Cross, and the Cross always leads on to the
Spirit.

CHAPTER III.

The Cross and the " So Great Salvation "

The third section of our diagram deals with the " so great salvation " (Heb. ii. 3); a phrase which at once sets forth its comprehensiveness and inclusiveness. Under that term we gather the various words which represent its many-sidedness: Substitution; Representation; Redemption; Justification; Reconciliation; Regeneration; Sonship; Sanctification; Glorification. The best way in which to see the significance and the peculiar value of each word or work is to ask one simple question. In what state does the word indicate man to be to make such a work necessary ?

I. Substitution

Man is clearly regarded as being totally unable to fulfil the Divine requirements as of himself. Those requirements would utterly destroy him and leave no residue of hope or prospect. He is judged and condemned and must die. But his death is more than physical, it is a state of con-

scious forsakenness of God, a consciousness to
which man is to awake sooner or later unless he
is saved—that is hell ! For only a few that hell
has really commenced in this life, for it is a part
of the Divine order that men should live here
under an aegis of mercy and grace. But " after
death the judgment " (Heb. ix. 27). Grace and
judgment belong to two dispensations. That is
why men presume upon God's grace. The
grand feature of the day of grace is that God
has—in the Person of His Son, Jesus Christ—
provided a Substitute, Who has taken man's
place in being " made sin on our behalf " (2 Cor.
v. 21), and has passed into that ' hour ' (which,
in its awfulness, is an eternity) of being forsaken
of God. " My God, My God, why has thou
forsaken me ? " (Mark xv. 34). That Substitute
is offered to men, for their faith acceptance of
Him—" the Lamb of God, that taketh away the
sin of the world." (John i. 29). That means that
when He died, He was accounted by God as
their sin, their judgment, their doom, their
death, their hell. It is as though they had borne
it all but are saved. It required a Substitute
Who, in Himself, was sinless, so that there was
that behind all upon which judgment had no
power and over which death and hell had no
rights. ' There was no other good enough to
pay the price of sin.' Hence God could raise
Him from the dead in virtue of His own inherent

sinlessness. This could never have been so with us. All that I was, Christ was made on the Cross for me. All that I was not that God required, Christ is unto me in resurrection. This, very briefly, is substitution.

II. Representation

But the fact that this has been done for me by another is only one side of the great work and could leave the door open to many weaknesses if it were left by itself. The complementary aspect is that of representation. " One died for all, therefore all died " (2 Cor. v. 14). In substitution, Christ died *for* us; in representation, He died *as* us. This means that, in the mind of God, we, as belonging to the old creation, have passed out of sight. When we take the Lord Jesus as our substitute and representative, we are regarded as in Christ and only so does God see us. When the Apostle Paul said " One died for all, therefore all died " (in Him), he went on to say, " that they that live should no longer live unto themselves, but unto him who for their sakes died and rose again." This means that we cannot take the substitutionary work of Christ and then just go on as though it had no relationship to what we are by nature. Moreover, it was not just our sin that He took, but ourselves; not what we call ' the bad ' about us, but our entirety.

The same Apostle came to see that this applied
to him as formerly a very religious man, consumed by a fire of religious devotion and activity. But the Cross represents the zero of the
old creation in all its aspects, nature and abilities,
and the beginning all anew as by resurrection
from the dead. It is significant and impressive
to remember that it was to Christian believers
that Paul expounded this truth as in the letter
to the Romans.

III. Redemption

The word ' redemption ' at once indicates its
own meaning. Man has been sold, or has sold
himself. Satan offered Adam a bargain (?),
blinding his mind to the real issues involved. In
unbelief and resultant disobedience in the matter
of a precise Divine instruction, Adam bartered
his soul for certain promised advantages, and
sold himself to Satan and sin, and the race with
him. In that position man has remained, and the
strength of it is that Satan has rights because
he has the ground of his own nature. Redemption means that those rights are undercut and
disposed of. That is done again in the Person
and work of the Lord Jesus in His Cross. The
great fact is that in Jesus Christ Satan has no
ground of authority because he has no ground
of nature. There he is " cast out " (John xii.

31). Satan's power of authority is death. The Lord Jesus "tasted death in the behalf of every man" (Heb. ii. 9), and met in Himself the final power of Satan, that "through death he might bring to nought him that had the power of death, that is, the devil" (Heb. ii. 14). Thus man is redeemed unto God and upon the redeemed man Satan no longer has any claims.

A sidelight upon this is found in a legal process by which a Greek slave obtained his freedom and preserved it, and it is to this well-known procedure that doubtless the Apostle Paul refers in Galatians vi. 17. The Greek slave, when he desired to secure his liberty, did not bring his master his earnings and obtain his freedom with his receipt for the money; he went to the temple of the god, and there paid in his money to the priests, who then with this money bought the slave from his master on the part of the god, and he became for the rest of his life a slave of the god—which meant practically freedom, subject to certain periodical religious duties. If at any time his master or his master's heirs claimed him, he had the record of the transaction in the temple. But on one point the records are silent. If he travelled, if he were far from home, and were seized as a runaway slave, what security could he have? It would seem that Paul gives us the solution. When liberated at the temple, the priest branded him with the "stigmata" of his new master. So Paul's words acquire a new meaning. He had been the slave of sin and of Satan; but he had been redeemed by Christ, and his new liberty consisted in his being the slave of Christ. 'Henceforth,' he says, 'let no man attempt to reclaim me; I have been marked on my body with the brand of my new Master, Jesus Christ.' The one flaw in this illustration is, of course, that no man can earn the means for his own redemption. Christ alone could provide this.

IV. Justification

Justification sets forth a standing or position to which the believer is brought. Each of the preceding steps relates and leads to justification. Substitution sees the sin question dealt with; representation sees the old creation removed and the new brought in; redemption sees the link with Satan and his kingdom destroyed. When these three things have been effected, then we have the answer to the question "How can man be just with God ? " (Job ix. 2), or, in other words, How can a man stand in the presence of God as just, or righteous ? The full answer is that we are justified in Christ Jesus. Through faith's acceptance of His substitutionary, representative, and redemptive work, we are now accepted in Him and are upon the wonderful footing of being regarded in the light of His perfections. He is made unto us righteousness from God. It is " the righteousness of (which is from) God through faith" (Rom. iii. 22). This position is an utter one from God's standpoint and must be so from ours. It is a position to be taken in its fulness by faith and maintained as a way in which to walk by faith. "The just shall live by faith" (Gal. iii. 11; Heb. x. 38). Satan will never cease to try to bring us back on to the old ground, and this he will do by ever bringing up to us what we are in ourselves and getting our eyes off Christ. His methods are countless, but the answer to them all is 'Not what I am, O Lord, but what Thou art,' and a strong holding on and looking off unto Jesus, the author and perfecter of faith.

V. Reconciliation

The justified are reconciled. In our natural condition, we were alienated from, and at enmity with, God, and indeed we *were* enmity against God. It only requires given conditions to bring out from every one of us some positive rebelliousness; but in Christ Jesus and His mighty reconciling work in His Cross, we who " were far off are made nigh" (Eph. ii. 13); we who were enmity are at peace. We are brought into the blessed fellowship of a new life and a new spirit.

VI. Regeneration

Regeneration is not something extra to what has gone before, but is a feature or factor in all. It puts its finger upon that which has taken place in us. By regeneration something is present which was not there before, a life from God which only the born-again possess, an indwelling of the Holy Spirit which is not true of any others. This Spirit of life in Christ Jesus has in it all the potentialities of a new creation in every part. There is a new consciousness, a new capacity, a new sense of relationships, a new direction, a new standard, a new vocation. Indeed, it is the birth of a new child. Everything is new and has to be learned from the beginning. We really know nothing of God's thoughts and ways and standards and purposes until we are regenerated. The freedom and fulness in which we move in our new life and all that it means will largely depend upon our recognition of what has gone before, and perhaps especially of our death and resurrection union with Christ, because here, in this new creation order, the old mentality has no place, and it is only to hamper the work of the Spirit in us if we persist in bringing over *our* ideas , *our* desires , *our* judgments, *our* choices, even if we think them to be in the interests of the Lord. We have to learn that the best of our old make-up may be all out of line with the simplest things of the Spirit of God. Regeneration is a new creation, and it is essentially *new*.

VII. Sonship

Sonship is something more than being born again. It represents growth unto fulness. It is quite a good thing to be a babe while babyhood lasts, but it is a bad thing to be a babe when that period is past. This is the condition of many Christians. Without going into technicalities, the New Testament in its original language makes a very clear distinction between a child and a son. While sonship is inherent in birth, in the New Testament sense sonship is the realisation of the possibilities of birth. It is growth to maturity. So the New Testament has a lot to say about growing up, leaving childhood and attaining unto full stature. With this growth comes the greater fulness of Christ and the abundant wealth into which we are saved. The so great salvation has its greater meaning for those who are going on unto full growth. In other words, it is a matter not so much of that *from* which we are saved, as of that *unto* which we are saved. The grand climax of the new creation is " the revealing of the *sons* of God " (Rom. viii. 19).

VIII. Sanctification

Sanctification again is an aspect and not necessarily an addition. Briefly, this indicates an act
and a process. Sanctification and consecration
are alternative and synonymous terms. Firstly,
they mean a setting apart or being set apart unto
God. The New Testament is quite clear that,
as we are justified in Christ by faith, so also we
are sanctified in Christ by faith, and that this
precedes the work of making us holy in ourselves.
Thus to believers who had many imperfections
the Apostle addressed his letter—unto " them
that are sanctified in Christ Jesus " (1 Cor. i. 2).
Thus, when we are in Christ, the Divine mind
concerning us is that we are wholly set apart
unto the Lord. We are as consecrated as anyone
can be as to our position. But the same Apostle
who refers to believers as already sanctified in
Christ Jesus, also writes to believers telling them
that his prayer for them is that they may be
sanctified wholly, spirit, soul and body (1 Thes.
v. 23). This simply means that what we are by
position has got to be made good in our state.
Sanctification or consecration is fundamentally
a matter of separation. With the Fall, an entang-
ling with another nature and order took place. It
became organic, therefore constitutional. The
Cross of the Lord Jesus cut right in between that
order and organism and a new and utterly dif-

ferent one as represented by Christ. Sanctification is, therefore, the working of the Cross in us to make good the nullification of that entangled nature and to bring in, in ever-increasing fulness, what Christ is as that ' altogether other.' In His simple language of illustration, it is taking up the Cross daily and denying ourselves (Matt. xvi. 24). But the fuller spiritual explanation of that, which is given us later in the New Testament, is the working of the Cross in us to bring an end to that self-life which is inextricably bound up with a system of evil. Thus, we being regarded as sanctified in Christ Jesus by faith, the process of sanctification is our experimental approximation to the position in which we are placed by the grace of God.

It will be seen that sanctification thus follows closely in the sequence of things and is based upon substitution, redemption, justification, reconciliation, regeneration, sonship.

IX. Glorification

In the case of the Lord Jesus, the suffering and glory are always kept together; suffering, the foundation ; glory, the topstone. Glorification is the spontaneous issue of the working in us of that Divine life, the incorruptible life of God. That life has in it all the potentialities of glorification. What has been said above is of two activities: —

    (*i*)   The setting aside of all that cannot be glorified.

    (*ii*) The bringing in of the new organism with the new life and its increase unto the fulness of Christ,

and this twofold work of the Cross leads on to glorification. Glorification begins in the spirit, that is, the renewed spirit of the child of God, by reason of the indwelling Spirit of glory, the Holy Spirit. Glorification proceeds as the soul—mind, heart, will; reason, desire, volition—is brought into subjection to the spirit and made its servant; in other words, brought under the Lordship of the Holy Spirit through our spirit. The consummation of glorification will be in the body, " to wit, the redemption of our body " (Rom. viii. 23), and " when this corruptible shall have put on incorruption " (1 Cor. xv. 54) then this mortal body shall have been made like unto His glorious body, or body of glory. Thus sonship will be completed as the out-working of regeneration; sanctification of spirit, soul and body will be the mark of perfect sonship, and glorification the issue.

Surely we are able, in the light of even this very brief and far from complete consideration of this great range of the work of the Cross, to endorse the term " so great salvation." We are also able to appreciate the seriousness of the warning, "How shall we escape if we neglect so great salvation ? " (Heb. ii. 3). God has covered every need and requirement and has compassed the whole ground from A to Z in the Person of His Son and the work of His Cross.

CHAPTER IV.

The Cross and the Lord's Coming Again

This is no more a treatise on the Second Advent of Christ than a former chapter was on the Holy Spirit. Our specific object is to point out the connection between the Cross and the Coming. This will be seen to be the fourth and final inter-section on our diagram.

Just as Salvation, Sanctification, the Holy Spirit, have been made something in themselves, and have become isolated doctrines, separated from their relatedness to all else, and have therefore become abnormal and unbalanced, so has it become with the teaching concerning the Lord's coming again. For a long time this matter fell into abeyance and was neglected or rejected. Then came a real awakening concerning it, and it was given its place again. But, like every swing of the pendulum, it has either taken on abnormalities, or become something in itself. In the one case it does positive harm: in the other it does not do much harm or good at all.

Some of us have lived long enough to outlive many Second Advent theories—not of cranks, extremists, or fanatics (although there have been some of these) but of honest, devout, and otherwise balanced and sound evangelical leaders. How sure some were that the German Kaiser was the Antichrist ! How much was published and said by prophetic students that Allenby's entrance into Jerusalem was the end of the times of the Gentiles ! Then Hitler took his place in the long line of Antichrists. A well-known evangelical leader travelled to Rome with the express purpose of telling Mussolini that he was the one raised up of God at the end-times to reconstruct the Roman Empire according to prophecy, and Mussolini took it on. Well, what about it all ?

We are not dismissing " signs of the times," for there undoubtedly are such, but we do emphasise that the spiritual aspect of things is far safer and more important than the temporal, fascinating as the latter may be. *Satan can sidetrack as much by means of unrelated truth as by positive error.*

Before his departure to be with the Lord, a beloved friend and servant of God who had made prophecy his life-long study, and who was well-known as an investigator, wrote to me and said that he had been compelled to change his entire standpoint and much of his interpretation in this whole matter. This is sad, if not tragic ! We do need to be on very safe and sure ground .

The Lord's Coming is Rooted in the Cross

and is the definite outworking as well as the outcome of it.

> ' Thou art coming; at Thy table
> We are witnesses for this.'

The Table, which shows forth His death, links
that death with His coming again—" till he
come."

To show that the Cross is the basis of the
Blessed Hope would be unnecessary here, but
to show *how* that is so may be important. The
reason for this is that so many have not got
beyond the idea—an idea never seriously thought
out—that the Second Advent is just an isolated
event, or an event which, standing in a pro-
gramme or time-table of dispensational movements, will just happen. When the clock strikes
twelve the Lord will come. Well, " within his
own authority " the Father may have the times
and the seasons, but in touching this matter we
are confronted with one of those inscrutable ways
of God. There are several of them in the Bible.
To reconcile freewill and predestination lies with
the wisdom of God alone, we cannot do it. In
the same way it is beyond our understanding
that a certain state which lies with the volition
of Christians should synchronise with a fixed
point of time for the Lord's coming. Yet it is

beyond dispute that in both the above matters the Bible is quite clear and emphatic. The Lord will come at a time definitely known to and fixed by Him, but, on the other hand, the Lord's coming will be just as much a spiritual matter as a chronological one.

It is on this spiritual side of Adventism that the Church and its teachers are so weak. As truly as Abraham's servant, sent to fetch the bride for Isaac, foreshadowed the Holy Spirit's being sent to fetch a bride for Christ, so truly is it a matter of spiritual progress on her part toward Him and the Spirit's showing of His things. Rebekah did not make one sudden leap from Mesopotamia to Canaan. It was a long, exacting and testing journey, and one involving a great exercise of faith. There was the whole question of leaving everything and everyone whose roots were in that land. There was the matter of implicit trust in the servant. There was, no doubt, a temptation more than once to wonder if the end was sure. And there was the constant battle with the reactions arising out of the weariness and the length of the unfamiliar way. But all this had a necessary effect upon this elect bride to both fit her for her great vocation and make the ecstasy of realisation all the greater. This is at best a poor figure of the spiritual side of the consummation of union with Christ at His appearing.

The fact is that we are to move just as much toward Him as He to us. The break with all here in a heart way, the leaving of this world spiritually, the occupation with the things of Christ, the patient endurance, and the growth of faith, are indispensable and inseparable factors in relation to His coming and our going on with Him.

Let there be differences of opinion as to the willy-nilly translation of Christians, or as to whether the whole Church will be caught up at Christ's coming; it is not necessary to formulate theories or teachings on such matters. Selectiveness of rapture may or may not be held, but from one thing no one can get away, God has left no room for theories here; a spiritual state of separation, occupation, and expectation is invariably bound up with our being received by Him at His appearing. Why argue otherwise and support a presuming upon the grace of God? Why take risks on a false idea of Grace when God has given us nothing but a positive demand, saying nothing whatever about His having a place for those who are less than one-hundred-per-cent going on with Him ?

In our diagram there are two blue lines, and blue stands for heavenliness. Israel in the wilderness were given a blue token to wear on the border of their garments. This betokened that they were—in God's mind—a heavenly people. They no more belonged to the wilderness than they did to Egypt. It was a place in which to know and prove their heavenliness—heavenly life, resource, guidance, etc.—and it was always pointing to " a heavenly country " which was really their own. But Jordan was the way in, the real point of crossing. And Jordan for ever represents the Cross of Christ. As the Red Sea represented what God did *for* them, so Jordan was the figure of a work consummated *in* them.

" Ephesians " is the counterpart of " Joshua "; it is " in the heavenlies in Christ," but the Holy Spirit took what was chronologically first—" Thessalonians "—and caused it to be placed after " Ephesians," as much as to say—The Coming of the Lord (the main theme of " Thessalonians ") is the outcome of the Church's arrival at its heavenly position.

More will be said on this when we deal with the Church in our next chapter, but here we want to underline the Divine revelation that the Cross separates us from this world, from this " flesh," from Satan's authority, and joins us to Christ, brings us on to heavenly ground, and constitutes us a spiritual people, and it is for such that the Lord will come. When David was driven out of his place by the usurper Absalom and his company, he exercised sublime wisdom and faith by sending back Abiathar with the ark into the

city. It was his own foothold there. It was
that which would always give him a place, even
where he was otherwise repudiated. And *to it* he
would return. It was his hold and his magnet.
The Lord will not just return as a matter of
course. He will come to and for something. It
is a love matter. He will come for His bride,
but it has to be mutual. " Them that have *loved*
His appearing." So the Cross is as much a part
of the consummation as it is of the initiation, and
by its operation in the life as a principle and
power the Lord will come for " a people prepared." This preparation relates to heart condition and not to mental apprehension of prophetic
truth.

CHAPTER V.

The Cross and the Church

Having dealt with the four intersections on our diagram—the Cross and the Person of Christ, the Holy Spirit, the So Great Salvation, and the Coming Again—we proceed to note that these pass into and through—in the first place—the circle marked the Church which is His Body.

Both in its teaching as to the eternal election of the Church and its present vocation, and also in the actual expression at the beginning of this dispensation, the Bible shows that the *first* sphere in which all the content and meaning of those four magnitudes finds expression is the Church. It is not our intention to deal with the analysis of each given in the diagram, but a glance at that analysis will do two things. It will show what each of the four means and contains, and it will explain the nature and vocation of the Church.

One thing must be said here, although it should be obvious: these four stand together, and unless they *are* kept as a whole the Church is not the Church of God's intention and purpose.

We shall come on this again later.

It is *in* and *by* the Church that God has eternally chosen to reveal the meaning of Christ —the Person of His Son. So also is it there that all the meaning and value of the Holy Spirit is to be embodied. The So Great Salvation is that which constitutes the Church, defining both its nature and its vocation. The coming again of Christ has its primary meaning *in* the Church. We repeat, to separate these from their right relation to the Church, to leave the Church out and to take the doctrines apart from it, is to render the doctrines disembodied spirits, with no actual and practical vehicle of demonstration or expression—something in themselves. To have something called the Church which does not *express* these four is to have a misnomer, a falsehood, a body without a spirit or personality, a plastic body without nerves or living expression.

The first main thing to say then is that

The Church is the Object of Divine Concern

in relation to Christ.

In the eternal counsels of the Godhead, when it was determined that the consummate issue of the intended created universe should be the summing up of all things in Christ, it was then decided that an elect Body—called the Church, which is His Body—should be the vessel and vehicle of His fulness, the complement of Him that filleth all in all: nothing less and nothing other than the Church. God has never stopped short at individuals, many or few, as related to Himself. He could have made a thousand Adams as easily as one, but He did not, because one Adam is generic and indicates many in one, the corporate life of many in one. This was the basic principle in Abraham, Jacob, David, Christ. Ignore or violate the corporate and organic principle embodied in the Church, and substitute an institution, an organisation, a fraternity, and you make the continuation beyond one generation a matter of the replacement of the worn parts of a machine, and not the reproduction of organic life. What is not the Church in its full Divine concept will only get so far and then live on its past, its tradition, its founder, and its publicity. There have been, and are, many such things which, because of a specific need (to which we refer later), have been blessed of God and cared for by Him, and which have become ministries in themselves within restricted limits. Beyond a certain point of value they are not organically reproductive; they are not sending forth in an *organic* way their seed to fully and livingly express the fulness of Christ. There have been so many of these things which, while valuable and owned of the Lord as a needed ministry for the hour, because of His love for them have been presented by Him with His fuller thought. This has represented a definite crisis. The issues have been no less than, on the one hand, adjustment unto enlargement and a new lease of life and value: or, on the other hand, because of unwillingness to see that God needed such changes, a quiet, steady, almost imperceptible loss of the old character and vitality, and either a closing down toward the end of the lifetime of the first instruments, or the formation of a Trust to carry on the work. So often it has become like the tent in Shiloh without the Testimony in it.

The Lord may bless, even raise up, instruments, ministries, to serve a specific purpose, to emphasise or recover a lost value, but there comes a time when He sees that the need has now arisen for the related feature and character to be recognised and accepted, and He sees to it that the light concerning this is present or available. Everything of future increase hangs in the balances of the reaction of those concerned and responsible. God will never ultimately stop short of His full thought—the Church. Herein lies one of the aspects of the relatedness of the Cross to the Church. Only as it is proved that the Cross has produced a true adjustableness and enlargement to all the thought of God can God go on with us *indefinitely*. It is fatal eventually to have a fixity of mind that because a beginning was so definitely of God it is fixed and will never have to be advanced upon and adjusted to the further things of God. God is not necessarily cancelling anything that has been owned of Him, but He would put it into its larger place. The fact is that, if God is going to have His full thought concerning the Church —even in a comparatively small company— because things are as they are now many adjustments will have to be made. It is no less than a life or death issue, a gain or loss question, and this is decided by the measure in which the meaning of the Cross has really been apprehended. All the tremendous significance of the " ifs " of the New Testament relate to this, not to salvation when the ' if ' is addressed to Christians.

This necessitates our saying something concerning which the Word of God teaches as to

What the Church Is

Because of its immense importance to the Lord's eternal purpose concerning His Son, there are few directions in which the great enemy has given himself more assiduously than in this to bring confusion, misapprehension, delusion, illusion, and disruption. The very fact that, on the one hand, the Church bears such evident marks of the Spoiler, and on the other hand, because of the confusion and mess so many true servants of God have turned to other than Church ministry in its full sense, should impress us with the significance of this matter from Satan's viewpoint. Nothing that implies the Church principles of corporate life—oneness, fellowship, and organic relatedness—fails to be the immediate object of Satanic interest and concern, to divide, confuse, and break up, and the devilish factor in it makes it more than just a matter of human disagreement. It is something much more subtle and difficult to deal with than that. The *real* trouble is not finally cleared up with apologies. In the light of this it *is* necessary to have some understanding and apprehension as to the true nature of the Church.

Of course, one of the governing things in deciding what the Church is is our standpoint. While the building with a spire or tower is so often called a church—and no one with any spiritual intelligence believes that it is—it will serve as an illustration of a major point. Supposing you saw such a building called a church standing on its spire with its main building right up where the top of the spire usually is, what would you say about it ? You would say two things. One: ' It is upside down.' The other: ' It is top heavy.' Perhaps you would say: ' It is absurd ! ' But that would entirely depend upon your standpoint. Supposing you were up

10,000 feet in an aeroplane and viewed it as
though the cloud-ceiling was your earth ? There
it would be right, and *it would be upside down
if in its usual position here.* It depends upon
whether our standpoint is earthly or heavenly.
From the standpoint of the New Testament—
which is " in the heavenlies "—the Church as it
is now on the earth is upside down. Its main
bulk is earthly, and its smallest point is heavenly.
I have no doubt that whoever invented the
church-steeple intended it to indicate that the
Church points to heaven, which, of course, is
true. But there is this other way of looking at
it. Really from God's standpoint the Church
has no connection with this world *in this dispensation* beyond testimony. It is *not* mainly pointing upward, but, being a heavenly thing, is
testifying downward. To link the Church with
this world at present in any other way is to
forfeit all that is really vital to its impact *upon*
the world. The Church therefore cannot be a
national thing, nor can it be international. There
is no such thing with God as the Chinese Church,
the Indian Church, the American Church, or
the English Church. The Church belongs to
no country. It can only be the Church *in* any
country or countries. Nor is the Church com-
posed of all nations or nationalities—Asiatics,
Americans, Europeans, etc. There " *cannot be
Greek and Jew* " in the Church. To think and

speak and act as though there were is to have failed lamentably to see God's thought as to the Church, and it *does* matter *very* much whether we are right or wrong in this.

In the same way, and belonging to a true apprehension of the Church, we must see that it can never be denominational, interdenominational, nor undenominational as such. A world federation of " churches " would altogether miss the Divine idea, and as lamentably break down in its spiritual value as did the League of Nations; it would be just another spiritual fiasco.

The Church *may* or *may not* be found somewhere inside *all* of the above, but it is other than they are.

It will be seen that, so far, we are on a negative line, and this has to be pursued a little further yet. There are sincere people of God who need to be reminded that the Church is not constituted upon some special line or measure of Divine revelation. Light as to the Church or the Body of Christ does not *make* those who have it the Church. The Church is not made by seeing a *fuller* meaning of the Cross or the Body. Important as this is in relation to *expression* it is not basic to the *fact*.

There are many other negative factors which affect this issue, but they will be covered as we proceed to the positive side. If we are actuated or influenced by the things as above mentioned, it is because we have not yet, after all, seen Christ.

The Church is for the Expression of Christ

Christ—the Son of God, the Son of man—is not a Jew in His resurrection person and humanity. Neither is He of any other nationality. He is altogether other. What nationality was the first Adam ? He was racial. In Christ God has gone back behind all these subsequent distinctions and differences, which the Bible attributes to Satan and rebellion, and He has gone beyond these to the grand issue when oneness will be absolute in every respect—Christ being all and in all actually and universally, as He *is now* where God's mind is concerned. For *God's* Church there is no ground but the ground of Christ. What is of ourselves by nature, and what is of this present evil world, is not the Church, for the Church is Christ corporately expressed. Spiritual understanding in this matter will result in our ceasing to talk about ' the Church of . . .' or ' Such-and-such a Church.' It will be absolutely revolutionary in mentality and issue in adjusted phraseology, but quite spontaneously, not pedantically or affectedly.

To have seen Christ as the Holy Spirit would show Him in the New Testament is to see that the Church begins by

Christ Becoming Resident in Believers

Once Christ is really within as a Resident a union has been established which is organic—in life—and that is Body union. The Lord's Table testifies to this and is for all true believers. That the full light on the Church had not been given in the first days of the Church as in " Acts " is evident, but the fact was there, and they continued " steadfastly in the breaking of bread." (See 1 Corinthians x. 16-17).

But the breaking and distributing of the loaf is never looked upon as making so many more loaves or bodies. It is still one loaf. Christ —though imparted to ten thousand hearts—is not ten thousand Christs, but still one. In this way the Church is Christ.

The growth of the Church is on the same principle. It is the increase of Christ, inwardly and extensively. The Church makes increase as Christ gets more room, or as the measure of Him increases in believers. Its outward growth numerically is just Christ getting into more lives (see Ephesians iv. 15-16). The measure of Christ determines whether the Church is strong or weak, great or small, effective or ineffective. But we must not confuse things. Firstly, we must not confuse Christ with systems which have grown up or been formed around Christ or the Church. Then we must not have a mental attitude that because certain believers are in these systems they are not the Church. This can be as divisive in effect as rabid sectarianism. Then we must not confuse the *fact* of the Church and the *expression* of it. This is where many trip up, and it is largely a reaction to the deplorable mixture and spiritual poverty of what is called ' the Church.'

The *fact* of the Church and its *expression* are two things. The fact is that all who are in *living* union with Christ—Who is Head—are the Church. I know that some teachers such as G. H. Pember do not agree with this, and I know all the problems which arise because of the position taken. How many problems would be solved and difficulties got over if we had a sufficient basis for believing that in this dispensation there are two things—the Church *and* the rest of believers ! We should, for instance, solve the problem of why so few respond to the testimony concerning the Church. But this will not do. The same problem lies behind why so many never make any response at all to Christ.

The expression of the Church, which is more than the fact, demands a recognition of the absolute Headship of Christ—that is, the doctrine lived out by the Holy Spirit. The Epistles did not put believers into a basic rela-

tionship with Christ; they revealed what that
relationship was and implied, and showed them
where they were as to this.   It is possible to
have a very crippled, emaciated, and unhealthy
body, so far as the outward frame is concerned,
but it cannot be said that it is not a body at all.
This is how it was in the *expression* of the Body
at Corinth.   Things could hardly have been
worse, and if we heard of such a state existing
in a local church to-day we should be sorely
tempted to write it off as having no vital relationship with Christ.   Paul did not do this with
Corinth; but writing to them as to the Church *in*
Corinth he just sought to show them Christ and
the corporate implications of Christ. It amounted
to a question as to the absolute Lordship of
Christ.

While all is completed in the ascended Christ,
all believers do not know what that ' all ' is, and
therefore may be failing in the expression. The
expression is of such value as to involve nothing
less than God's eternal purpose and satisfaction;
and, as we have said, the utmost wrath of Satan
is directed against any ministry which leads to
this, or any expression of the Church in spiritual
reality.   It is no less an issue than Christ coming
fully into His place, and Satan having no more
room.

It is therefore of utmost importance that there
should be light as to the Church—the Body.

Strength or weakness, we repeat, depends upon this. This is

Where the Cross Comes In

Christ cannot come in until man goes out. This applies initially and progressively. There is no place in Christ for the fallen and Satan-produced judgments, thoughts, energies, feelings, etc., of another man. The measure of Christ depends upon the exit of what is not Christ. This has to be faced as a basic and inclusive fact sooner or later, once for all. Then it has to be recognised that conformity to the image of Christ is a life-process, and this life-process goes on on the basis of the Cross. It is not new dyings of Christ, it is not a repetition of the Cross, once, twice, or many times, but it is an outworking of the once-for-all meaning and implications of the Cross. The presence and effect in the Church of what we are naturally is to limit Christ, and therefore to deny the Church, and therefore to counter the Sovereign Headship of Christ, and therefore to make for spiritual weakness, and *therefore* to put Satan in the place of power. All this is met by the Cross of Christ. Hence, the Altar stands at the threshold of the House; it is the big Altar—a *whole* burnt-offering. The Cross takes its greatness from the immensity of that to which it relates, and makes possible, in the eternal counsels of God.

If what we have said above raises practical questions for any as to relationship and connections, etc., we do not say that you should do this or that—leave this, join that. All that we say is—Look the Cross fully in the face once more, ask the Lord to show you what it means in His fullest thought, let the Lord Jesus be absolutely Head, meet the challenge, and be obedient to what He shows you.

CHAPTER VI.

The Cross and the Church (Continued)

In our consideration of the Church we have on several occasions used the word "expression," thus noting the difference between the heavenly conception and nature, and the practical application. This latter is of very great importance, and it is here that we find all the reactions of God against declension and failure down the ages. The *whole* Church on earth may not come to a true and full expression of God's thought as to its nature—it never has done since the very first days—but God has never accommodated Himself to this failure and given some intimation that He will be satisfied with whatever He can get. He holds to His full mind, retains the full revelation of it in the New Testament, seeks to have as many in the good of it as will pay the price, and determines *spiritual* measure accordingly, while blessing all that He can that contributes to it.

We are therefore bound to say something regarding the expression of the Church in this universe; for we must remember that the Church is more than earthly, it is cosmic. Its accountability extends even now " unto the principalities and powers in the heavenlies " (Eph. iii. 10). If, as we have said, the Church is Christ in corporate expression we shall best apprehend this practical aspect of its calling by considering its correspondence to Christ.

Christ Spiritually Expressed

When we turn to see how Christ was here spiritually, we find that it was mainly in terms of three great forces and impacts—life, light, love. Just to say this is, for the average reader of the New Testament, to bring up no small material which bears it out.

" In Him Was Life "

Life is the supreme issue of the Bible, and therefore of creation. The Bible opens with the Tree of Life and it closes with the same. Everything between, as covering the whole history of creation, is focused upon this issue. It is one long continuous conflict concerned with this one question. If the Old Testament is, as Christ said it was, a testifying to Him in all its parts, the issue is found in Christ risen, triumphant over death. The Church's preaching in the book of the " Acts " is little more than a proclamation of the resurrection of the Christ. Thus Christ is the comprehensive and all inclusive embodiment of death's destruction and life victorious. The

Church as His Body takes up this testimony, not firstly doctrinally or verbally, but actually and factually. It is intended to be the carry-on of Christ in this respect. Not to historic events nor to New Testament teaching does she first bear her witness, but she is to *be* the very embodiment of Christ in terms of life.

There are three ways in which life is manifested.

(1) Life is Generic

The Divine principle of the creation is biological. Life is the key to everything. When God put life into things He not only set a course in motion which would work itself out apart from outside stimulants and direction, but He introduced the potentialities of perfect development according to the particular kingdom to which the organism belonged—human, animal, vegetable, etc. Life produced after its own kind, but life *produced*. The battle for life and of life started when sin entered ; but whatever the changes, life still forces on and keeps the creation going. So in the spiritual realm, life is the key to everything, and the only justification for the continuance of this creation. The Church, for which all things are summed up in Christ, takes its origin from His resurrection, and therefore the implanting of

His triumphant life. ' She is His new creation,' and He is her new creation life. Her very existence rests upon His risen life. She will eventually be judged by Him Who stands before her and says, " I am . . . the Living one; and I became dead, and behold, I am alive for evermore." Not sound doctrine alone ; not much activity; not a high standard of moral integrity; but life, death-conquering, hell-vanquishing life, will be the test.

(2) Life is Energic

The driving force of the Church is the power of life. In Ezekiel's vision of the Cherubim and the wheels, a symbol of Christ and the Church, the driving force was the Spirit of life. It is a picture of energy. Going, going, ever going, ceasing not, and straight forward. It is the Living Ones (not " beasts " or " creatures ") in corporate expression. It is not difficult to see the correspondence between this as a symbol and the actual spiritual counterpart in the Church at the beginning. Life took charge, or the Spirit as the Spirit of life took charge, and the goings were with much energy. Testimony, evangelism, mutual concern, and many other things betokened life. It was not man-made zest, enthusiasm, emotion, drive, or momentum. It was accounted for by no external stimulant being administered. Such would need to be kept up by outside means, but this was spontaneous and transcended all obstacles.

When we read of " the power that worketh in us," or " working in us that which is well-pleasing," or " his working, which worketh in me mightily," the word in the Greek is " energy," " energiseth," " energising." It is the energy of Divine life by the Holy Spirit, and is so frequently set over against much human frailty and infirmity, thus constituting a mighty testimony to " the power of his resurrection." There is nothing to account for the persistence and accomplishments of the Church but the supernatural energy of the Divine life in her, and this is the testimony for which she exists. You have to look deeper into the Jesus of Nazareth, the Man of Galilee, for an explanation of His impact upon this world through so long a time, and you will find the secret in the life which was in Him and which He imparts in new birth. In the same way the Church's secret should always be deeper than her outward form ; it should be the energy of nothing less than the very life of God in her.

(3) Life is Reproductive

This is *the* meaning of life. It may mean joy, energy, beauty, and activity, but its essential value and supreme function is reproductiveness. Life demands a way to reproduce after its kind, and any organism which refuses right-of-way to life by denying its facilities for transmission commits a breach of trust. Nowhere is life a possession just to be enjoyed. It is a stewardship to be sacredly fulfilled. The barren fig-tree of Matt. xxi. is a parable of an unfulfilled trust ; receiving without passing on. Possess life, and give it a free course and reproduction is spontaneous. This is not only the statement of a fact, it is a test. The New Testament Church, or the Church in the New Testament, was a spontaneously reproductive Church, without machinery, organisation, publicity, propaganda. It propagated itself purely by reason of the life in it. There are many substitutes for Divine life in organised Christianity which explain the slow and hard going, expensive output, and poor quality of results. There is no real substitute for the Church, and the Church expressing Christ as "seeing his seed" in terms of spontaneous reproduction of life. There is something irresistible about life and the most serious consequences are attached to attempts to thwart it. Christ—the Life—is *just simply bound* to come out with a great multitude at the end.

But this life-productiveness is by way of the Cross. The classic Scripture on this is John

xii. 24. The grain of wheat dies to reproduce itself. Christ Himself brought His Church into being thus. So that corporate expression of Christ is not only by *His* death, but potentially the death of all, and the truly living ones are those who have been " raised together with him." This is the Church, and the continuation of reproduction is the continuation of the faith acceptance of death and resurrection union with Him, with all that God means by that.

" The Life was the Light "

In the order of the new creation, that is, of what is spiritual, light follows life ; life precedes light. Nicodemus was a man in the dark, groping. Christ said to him " Except a man be born anew he cannot *see*." Light is the great seeing factor ; therefore it means knowing, perceiving, being sure. Inasmuch as it comes through life it must be subjective, inward. The man born blind (John ix.) who received his sight is a full scale example or type of this. The touch of Jesus communicated life, vital power. He saw. Then, over against every effort to undermine his faith, to prejudice his mind, he simply answered that he had the goods and that was what really mattered. There was no merely doctrinal argument. It was not a matter of a certain line of teaching or angle of truth. It was Christ in terms of living light. He not only had light on things, he had *sight*. It was not information *about*, but it was apprehension *of* !

What a challenge to the Church this is ! Christ is not theories, interpretations, doctrines, speculations, information, themes, etc. Christ is the impact of light upon darkness, so that ' the darkness overcometh him not.' This is exactly what a corporate expression of Christ is ; *is*, not should be. The Church, when in her true place and relationship to Him, *is* this. It can be as truly so with her as it was in His own case.

Much could be written regarding the effect of light, but here we are only stating spiritual facts, and leaving it with those concerned to do the measuring up. When the sun shines in its power it is not necessary to discuss theories about light, and if you do, it is only in the nature of explaining something which already exists. Nine-tenths of Christian teaching to-day has to do with what would follow, obtain, result, if certain things happened ; or in explaining what would happen if certain things were observed. There is *very* little call for explaining what is happening, answering the enquiry, " What meaneth this ? " with " This *is* that . . . " And yet it ought to be this way. New Testament doctrine was mainly an explanation of what had happened. It is important as light upon life, but the fact of the Church's being in the place where this life is bringing forth enquiry as to her secret is really where she begins her ministry. So it was on the Day of Pentecost. See what a tantalizing enigma Christ was when here. " Whence hath this man this wisdom ? " Not of the schools, the seats of learning, nor the books, but in fellowship with the Father, under the anointing of the Spirit, He saw what the Father was doing (John v. 19). The Church should be just the same; baffling the unbelieving, defeating the curious, leaving the prejudiced with *facts*, and being light to the true seekers.

But she will have to undergo a deep crucifixion to her own wisdom as to how the work of God is done. There is no light on the death side of the Cross where man by nature is shut out from God. She will have to cry in her blindness, " Jesus, thou Son of David, have mercy on me." This brokenness, helplessness, hopelessness, and yet faith, will betoken her death to every resource but Him Who is the life and the light of man. The Cross governs this whole matter of the Church's testimony to the light.

The Love of Christ

It seems hardly necessary to gather up what

is in the New Testament to show that, like as Christ was here as the life and light of men, so He was here as the embodiment and expression of the love of God. This is all so well known. In the same way it would be unnecessary to cite the much Scripture which shows that it is by that love that the Church proves Him to have been sent of God (John xvii. 21).

There are, however, some things in this connection which need fresh emphasis, if not an indicating of their implications. Seeing that we are dealing with the Church and the Cross, we can find all that is necessary in that part of the New Testament where this is brought to its fullest expression. In the letter to the Ephesians it is most impressively made clear that even

Light is Based Upon Love

" *Ye, being rooted and grounded in love, may be strong to apprehend* . . . (*iii.* 17, 18).

Earlier in the letter we have these words: " *having the eyes of* your heart *enlightened* . . ." (*i.* 18). Then what immense things follow as to be known by the Church ! We do not dwell upon them, but upon this fact, that light, knowledge, is the fruit which springs from rooting in love. It would seem that God only gives — but gives abundantly — spiritual knowledge to those whose main characteristic is love. Love for Him, yes ! but love for His own and for all men.

" *I love the Father* " (*John xiv.* 31).

" *The Father loveth the Son and sheweth him all things* . . . " (*John v.* 20). So Christ attributed His own knowing all things from the Father to mutual love between them. But Christ was the personal embodiment and manifestation of God's love for the elect and for the world (John iii. 16 ; xvii. 23). (See also Eph. v. 25.) John is known as the Apostle of love. What a wealth of spiritual light has come to us through him ! Paul was behind no one in this matter of Divine love and has given us the classic of all time as to it (1 Cor. xiii). What fulness and depths of revelation the Church owes to him !

A scientist may describe a tear in terms of water, salt, and mucus, but the mother or lover *understands* it in terms of its real meaning. A head knowledge is no knowledge at all in spiritual values. Only the knowledge which comes through the heart—travail, suffering, longing, heart-break over souls, toward the Lord—is vital knowledge. How much of the wealth of knowledge possessed by John, Paul, and others came out of their heart travail for the Church ? Take that out, and there is not much left.

Love Buildeth Up

" . . . *the increase of the body unto the building up of itself in love* " (*Eph iv.* 16).

You might not have thought of that when considering the material for building the Church. Truth, yes ! Teaching, yes ! Knowledge, yes ! But the Holy Spirit singles out *love* for the main emphasis. Ephesus evidently stood for something in the matter of spiritual values. The fact that the Holy Spirit was so unrestrained in giving such light, light exceeding anything else in the whole Bible, is a fairly good proof of capacity. How well we know that when we minister in the Spirit we have liberty or restraint governed by the spiritual capacity of our hearers. We would often go further, but we just cannot. It comes back at us. At other times or places we can go all the way. Paul was just caught away with superlatives which piled themselves one upon another when he wrote that letter. The longest sentence without a full period in the Bible is found there. He could not stop for the rules and regulations of punctuation. Surely the explanation of this release of the Lord is found in His address to Ephesus in the Revelation (ii. 4)—" *Thou didst leave thy first love.*" " *Thy first love.*" There must have been something very precious to the Lord at the beginnings of the church in Ephesus. It is like the cry and sob of a broken-hearted lover, whose love moves into jealousy and heat against the detractor and the unfaithfulness. He sees the triumph of the " god of this world " in blinding the mind, and is angry with Ephesus for complicity with him. Well, much, very much, can be added on this matter, but enough ! Remember that the way in which the Church will be built inwardly and outwardly will not be alone by meetings, conferences, addresses, teaching, nor by campaigns, but by the bathing of all in love, and sometimes just pure love without lectures.

But—and is it necessary to say it ?—this love is the fruit of a deeply crucified life. It is only in a true and adequate apprehension and appreciation of the Cross that the heart is enlarged to *all* men. 'Love to the loveless.' It is only as the Cross has struck deeply at the roots of pride, personal interest, ambition, reputation, selfishness, and concern for something less than the whole purpose of God, that God will really build His Church. The Church is the Lamb's *wife*. It is a *love* matter! These two are one. She takes her very object in life from Him. She leaves all personal and former interests and relationships, and they two become one flesh.

" *As he is, even so are we in this world.* " This oneness has been wrought by the Cross in which they were made one in death, burial, resurrection and ascension.

CHAPTER VII.

The Cross and the Nations

Having seen that the first sphere in which the Cross has its expression in its various relationships is the Church, we now come to its place in the nations of the world. It must be recognised at the outset that, in the intention of God, the Cross does not pass *through* the Church to the nations, but takes the Church with it there. It is not the Cross in the nations as something preached apart from the Church, but the Church in the nations as the embodiment of the Cross. This cannot be represented in one diagram, therefore it has to be stated.

It is true that the Apostles preached among the nations Christ crucified and risen, but as a rule and a principle they did not do this single handed. The Lord's principle of a minimum of two was adhered to as closely and continuously as possible, and on the few occasions when an Apostle was isolated and alone there was usually hold up and threat either to ministry or life. This corporate principle of going forth as on 'Body' ground, with the Church behind, and the Church implied in more than one being together, indicated that the Lord's required means is that which represents Christ corporate. Two is regarded in the Bible as the number which implies adequate testimony. This is easily verifiable by a glance at the way in which two were joined by God so frequently, and that "in the mouth of two witnesses" everything shall be established. Now, then, the Lord had said "this gospel of the kingdom shall be preached in the whole world *for a testimony . . .* and then . . . the end . . ." The Church is the vessel of witness or testimony, hence the minimum is two. The principle is to have a corporate expression or representation of Christ in every nation. The deepest meaning of "evangelize" is to bring to, not only to proclaim. It is inherent in the word, and it means—to bring Christ to the nations. 'This good news of the realm and reign (of God through Christ) must be set in the nations for a testimony'; that would be the meaning of the statement. It is in keeping with all the fundamental principles of Divine revelation.

(1) "The Earth is the Lord's"

But the earth has become overrun and possessed by that which is inimical to God. He has been driven out, and a usurper has occupied the throne here. That is both stated and illustrated many times in Scripture.

After the flood, when the earth appeared as a purged and renewed thing, Noah and the nucleus of that new creation built an altar and consecrated the earth to God in that way ; in effect saying, " The earth is the Lord's." The testimony was locally represented ; a universal right locally established in a corporate company by what symbolised the Cross. When David was driven from his rightful place by the usurper Absalom, he sent Zadok back with the ark. Zadok and Abiathar were there with the testimony to the fact that David's rightful place was *there*, where the testimony was. The Church, with the testimony of Jesus, is to be representatively holding the earth for its rightful Lord.

(2) " All Things Have Been Created . . . Unto Him "

The nations are Christ's inheritance. "*Ask of me, and I will give thee the nations for thine inheritance, and the uttermost parts of the earth for thy possession.*"

The Church is the company in which Christ is establishing His right by taking an earnest of the inheritance. The nations may not be saved in this dispensaton, but they will yield a token, and in that ' people out of the nations for his name ' (Acts xv. 14) they declare that all is His by right. It is something, even if there are no mass movements, just to hold the ground for Christ. This will indicate the place of the Cross, for it was by it that He cast out the prince of this world. It was by it that He established His moral right to it. It was because of it that He was given " all authority in heaven and on earth," and received " the name which is above every name." Only in the virtue of Calvary's triumph shall we be able to hold our ground in this sin- and devil-ridden world.

Then, if this is true and the corporate principle is the effectual one, the one object of Satan, in order to frustrate the end and spoil the testimony, will be to break up the corporate life. Satan will never stop until he has done all that he can to divide the last two who are spiritually related in the testimony of Jesus. This will necessitate a deep work of the Cross in those concerned, so that ' the prince of this world will have nothing in them.' Humility, meekness, self-emptying, and deep devotion to the Lord's honour are fruits of the Cross. We cannot meet and counter Satan with doctrine, technique, phraseology and slogans about Satan being a defeated foe. He must meet crucified men and women who have given Christ a lot of room. You will see the corporate action of the

Church in the Book of the Acts. A 'Church' in the nations which is not crucified to the world is a help to Satan, but a crucified company is a great menace to his kingdom.

CHAPTER VIII.

The Cross and the Satanic Kingdom

Following closely upon what we said at the end of our last chapter, we come to the place and meaning of the Cross in the realm of principalities and powers, world rulers of this darkness, and hosts of evil spirits in the heavenlies (Eph. vi. 12).

Again, we must bear in mind that it is in and by the Church that the Cross has its registration in that realm. It is always a dangerous thing for units of the Church, i.e., individuals, to assail that kingdom, or enter it with intent to upset it. Christ alone can meet that, or to Him only as its conqueror will it yield, and, we repeat, Christ is implied by the corporate means. There is much spiritual history, both glorious and tragic, bound up with this principle, its observance or its neglect or violation. The whole matter of Headship is involved in this. Headship has never been relegated or delegated by the Lord to any individual. Autocracy or individual domination in the Church is a positive violation of the Church's major principle—the Sovereign

117

Headship of Christ. Hence 'the oversight' in the New Testament was always plural, never singular; elders, not an elder. In so far as authority was concerned it was corporate, not individual.

This does not mean that New Testament technique rigidly adhered to will result in a mighty impact of Christ's Headship of all principalities and powers. History proves otherwise. But this failure does not prove the principle to be false, it only shows that it is more technique than *spiritual* position.

But to come to our main subject of which such points are but the outworking, the inclusive thing about which we must be quite clear is that the ultimate place of the Cross is in that realm from which the Cross takes its original rise. The Cross is set at the very heart of

A Cosmic Struggle for the Mastery of the Creation

We use the word Cosmic in the sense of super-earthly. It embraces the earth, the heavenlies around the earth, and beyond. Here we find ourselves outside of time in eternity, outside of the local in the universal. There is an aspect of the Cross which is beyond atonement. Atonement has to do firstly with time and this world. It relates to man's sin and reprobation.

But atonement is not for Satan and "the angels that kept not their own principality" (Jude 6). The last thing that the Bible says about the former is that he is cast into the lake of fire "unto the ages of the ages" (Rev. xx. 10). (The same phrase is used of the glory of God in the Church [Eph. iii. 21]. The one is the counter-part of the other, and must be of the same duration.) Of the fallen angels it is said that they are "kept in everlasting bonds under darkness unto the judgment of the great day" (Jude 6) and "cast down to hell . . . to pits (or chains) of darkness, to be reserved unto judgment" (not salvation) (II Pet. ii. 4).

When we speak of a cosmic struggle for the mastery of creation, some might find it difficult to contemplate the infinite, almighty, eternal God involved in a struggle, as though He could not, with a word, a stroke of His hand, wipe out of existence everything that gets in His way. To overcome this mental difficulty, we must remember that the creation rests upon a moral foundation. In creation God has bound Himself to moral conditions, and has therefore brought Himself to the place where His authority operates only on moral grounds. He intervenes *for salvation* only when He has the ground which is in accord with His own moral nature. If the ground is positively and incorrigibly antagonistic to His moral nature, His interventions have been, and will be, unto judgment and destruction. Justification by faith has its place here in that God has provided or secured the ground of His own moral perfection in His Son, Jesus Christ, and that ground is provided for faith in Him. Persistent and final rejection of Christ and God's righteousness in Him puts those concerned into another realm, to which the Apostle Paul referred when he said " Knowing therefore the fear of the Lord, we persuade men " (II Cor. v. 11). (This word " fear " is strong ; really—' to terrify.') Just as God must have suitable ground for the beneficent exercise of His authority and power, so must Satan have ground suitable to his nature to exercise his authority. Take God's ground from Him and He cannot work for you. Give Him His ground, and He moves. All the meaning of *power through sanctification* lies here. " He did not many mighty works . . . because of their unbelief." Likewise, give Satan *his* ground and his authority is established. Take his ground away and he is helpless. Hence his one object, in order to establish his kingdom, is to corrupt, for then he knows that God cannot save ; it is a moral issue. So the battle is waged, not between two potentates on official and personal grounds, but between two moral orders represented by two lords, of righteousness and unrighteousness respectively.

It is in this direction that the Cross goes beyond atonement and puts the Church in the strong position of moral and spiritual authority in the realm where the evil forces have their seat. 'By the Cross He conquered.' That was because the Cross took Satan's moral ground from him.

The Church is a heavenly Body; which means that it is out of Satan's domain spiritually and morally. Delivered . . . out of the *authority* of darkness, and translated . . . into the kingdom of the Son of his love " (Col. i. 13). For its spiritual authority the Church *must* stand in all the good of the Cross as a separating and sanctifying power. Satan's one aim is to corrupt the Church. The wrestling against principalities and powers (Eph. vi. 12) is not physical, it is not to *obtain* a position of ascendency, it is against the " *wiles* of the devil." These wiles are twofold; to obtain a lodgment for darts of accusation—that is a denial of our justification and righteousness by faith: and, or, to corrupt and seduce on to earthly, carnal, and unholy ground. This explains the spiritual and moral nature of the armour provided.

The Church does not carry the Gospel of salvation and atonement to the kingdom of Satan itself, but only to those who are his prisoners, to give them the option of deliverance or remaining with him. To the evil powers the

Church stands to express the moral Lordship of Jesus Christ in virtue of His Cross, and to exercise that authority in virtue of its own standing in Him.

The position is this. Before the world was, God purposed to gather under one Head all the creation. That Head was His Son. It was irrevocably and unalterably settled in the eternal counsels. Knowing that it could never be its best by mere compulsion or as a mechanical order and that faith, love, and positive holiness (not passive innocence) were essential to that best, and foreseeing the advent of evil, a working of a subversive system, He provided against the ultimate triumph of the system in "the Lamb slain from the foundation (lit: the laying down) of the world." All that was foreseen, and the Lamb came out of eternity into time, was literally—not potentially—slain, the ground of the evil power was taken in that slaying, and the link-up renewed with the original purpose—" all things in Christ." The Church — the elect Body — was brought into being on the ground of the Cross. He was given to be " head over *all things to* (not merely *of*) the Church which is his body, the fulness of him that filleth all in all " (Eph. i. 22-23). The Church moved out and registered His rights behind the temporal and sentient world, in the spiritual kingdom of Satan, and it worked ! —

until the Church declined from its spiritual and heavenly position. The Cross is still the moral battle-axe of the Church, and the evil system can still feel its overthrowing power. It rests with the Church to adjust to

1. The meaning of the Cross;
2. The place into which the Cross puts the Church;
3. Positive aggression in its whole armour.

Our object has not been to deal at any length with the connected matters. Each one of them could easily fill a book to itself. We have aimed at indicating the place which the Cross has in all things related to God's eternal and universal purpose in Christ.

There remains but one realm indicated on our diagram. But before we pass to consider that, we would add something to this chapter with the object of doubly emphasing that power is a matter of position.

Position and Power

Undoubtedly the word which occurs most often in religious—and especially evangelical—circles to-day is the word " power." In addresses and prayers it is the keynote from which and to which there is constant movement. All the world over it is the same.

Listening to speakers and prayers in languages

with which one is not conversant, a certain word occurs with almost monotonous reiteration, and on inquiry one is not surprised to learn that it is this word. The absence of power and the necessity for it is betrayed or confessed in many ways ; not only directly and humbly by the more spiritually minded among God's people, but by the loud display of ingenious resourcefulness in advertisement, " stunts," organisation, drives, etc., which are a more sad giving-away of the case than what is meant to be implied by them, viz. : — that there is no life.

We do not intend to embark upon a consideration of this subject in general from all of its angles, but to deal with one basic thing, more basic even than the reception of the Holy Spirit. The matter is very rarely dealt with in relation to the Holy Spirit, and certainly no treatise can be anything like complete otherwise. The Master made it very clear that before there could be a Pentecost there were certain very deep and vital things to transpire. Pentecost was to be very truly an effect, and not only a cause ; the end of much as well as a beginning ; a seal and not only a pledge. Before there could be the counterpart of Christ's Jordan anointing upon the members of His Body, the Church, there must of necessity have been a baptism into His death, a union with Him in the entombment of the " body of sin." His death had meant the closing of the door upon the old creation ; the first Adam had been dealt with and effectually relegated to the place where he would no longer have any consideration or acceptance from God, being reckoned as dead, and only the inclusive " last Adam " would receive the fulness of God. In the day of the anointing of the servants of God of old, very definite and explicit instructions were given in relation to the anointing oil. This holy oil was in no wise to come upon man's flesh and there was to be no attempt to make anything like it.

The oil is always a symbol of the Holy Spirit, and the " flesh " a type of the old fallen nature of " Adam." God strictly refuses that the Holy Spirit should come upon uncrucified men and women. " Becoming conformed unto his death " is the only path to power. All our motives in seeking power will be tested by fire. Are we seeking personal influence, popularity, reputation, prestige, acceptableness, success, demonstrations, something of a kingdom of this world ? We may think our motive to be perfectly pure ; but not until we pass into death, death to any or all of the above, and find ourselves " despised and rejected of men," our names cast out as evil, and a real hold-up (seemingly) of our work, do we really come to face the real purpose and motive of our having any place in the work of God. The death or the eclipse of everything within and without is a good test. Many of the men of God who have been *truly* used by Him have gone this way. Not upon our flesh—whether it be the gross flesh or the refined, soulish, educated flesh—will God allow His Spirit to come. Before there can be a Pentecost there must have been a Calvary. Before there can be the fire of God there must be an altar and a sacrifice ; and it must be the *burnt* offering, in which everything is consumed. Undoubtedly the disciples of our Lord went through the death of everything of ambition, expectation, vision, self-confidence, etc., when their Master was crucified, and then they tasted deeply of that death which was to govern them all the days which were to be. Their views, ideas, " convictions," methods, scales of values, standards of judgment, dispositions, tempera- ments, personal influence and every part of their life, came under this government, and in every deeper baptism into death they were raised more fully into His life—not their own. Each experience was more critical and crucial and devastating than the last, and doubtless they sometimes wondered if there would be anything at all left ; but so the life was becoming more abundant. See for example Acts x, and II Cor. i. 8-10, etc.

This was and is the initial position which alone means power, and any seeming power which is not resultant from the ¡deep death of the natural life of the individual or community is a making of oil like unto the true but which is not the true, and therefore in the deepest sense is not the anointing of God. But there is a further element in this matter of position. In the world and the flesh Satan had judicial rights. These judicial rights and the ground of Satan's claim Christ came to deal with ; to destroy the ground and to possess Himself of the rights. In the light and the power of His Cross—which He had accepted at His baptism—and on the ground of His predestined position as the God-chosen " Prince of this world," Christ possessed a mystic authority ιwhich was recognised in every sphere and always set over against another authority. The Greek word *exousia*, translated in the A.V. " power " and in the R.V. " authority," would be more accurately translated " jurisdiction." See the recognition of this superior jurisdiction, for instance, in Matthew vii. 29, where it is set over against that of the scribes; in Matthew viii. 9, where it is above that of the Roman Empire behind the Centurion ; in Matthew xxi. 23, where the Pharisees betray their recognition of this mystic thing. The ninety-four occurrences of this word in the New Testament are very illuminating. Satan claimed the jurisdiction of the world, (Luke iv. 6). Christ did not deny his claim then, but went to the

Cross crying, "Now shall the prince of this world be cast out"; and having dealt with Satan and all the ground of his claim, Christ rose triumphant saying, "All jurisdiction has just been given to me in the heavens and on earth; for this reason go *ye* into the whole world and proclaim the good news" (Matt. xxviii. 18, 19, Lit. Trans).

In the light of this triumph and because He held this position in Himself He had said to His disciples, "Behold I have given you jurisdiction . . . . over all the power (*dunamis*—driving-force) of the enemy," (Luke x. 19). After His having possessed Himself of this jurisdiction on behalf of the race—as He possessed it in Himself as the Son of God—He promises them that they shall receive power (*dunamis*—driving-force) when the Holy Spirit is come upon them, Acts i. 8. There can never be "dunamis" until there is "exousia," that is, there can never be *driving-force* until there is *position.*

God will only put His power behind those who are in the authoritative position, and none are there who have not been incorporated into Christ in death, burial, resurrection, ascension, and reign, and this as a present *spiritual* experience. The jurisdiction of Christ through His Cross has to function through the members of His Body in concert. Christ has the jurisdiction, we are incorporated into Him if we have on all points accepted and claimed our identification with Him, and thus we have become the instruments of that authority over the driving-power of the enemy in every sphere where His victory is not recognised. By a life in the Spirit we are able to receive by discernment those indications from above—the " Head " —and then command the situation and put the enemy's work out of action. The word " destroy " in the New Testament means " put out of action," and this is related to " the works of the devil," and progressively wrought out on the ground of Calvary by " the church which is his body." This is not vulgar exorcism, for it can only be effectual as the Holy Spirit takes the initiative in us and through us, and we must know His " energising." Undoubtedly it was their absolute union with their victorious Lord, and the recognition of their judicial authority— not over men but over Satan and his kingdom— which was the ground of the Holy Spirit's seal and anointing of the Apostles and first believers. Galatians ii. 20 is for ever the key to the situation.

CHAPTER IX.

The Cross and the Heavenlies, "Far Above All"

Perhaps one of the most mysterious statements in the Bible is that made by Paul in the "Ephesian Letter" (iii. 10) that

> "*now unto the principalities and the powers in the heavenlies might be made known through the church the manifold wisdom of God.*"

At least it implies that the Apostle had been given a very special revelation, for this is one of the things that could never be arrived at by study, reasoning or deduction. What it all means we do not know, but we can see something.

Firstly, we find it difficult to believe that these principalities and powers are the same as those mentioned in Eph. vi. Why the Lord should want to display His manifold wisdom to the evil powers would indeed be hard to understand. If His all-governing object is the expression and diffusion of His glory in the universe so that worship comes back to Him in adoration, wonder, and amazed rejoicing, then we have the clue to this statement. The Church here is represented

130

as seated together with Christ in the heavenlies, not in the realm of the evil powers, but above them, amongst the angelic hosts. There, intelligences having absolute confidence in the wisdom and ability of God are nevertheless capable of being instructed and learning. They are aware of the unspeakably great and immense problems that have arisen through Satan's interference and man's complicity with him—the problems of man's disrupted and twisted nature; of the resultant power of Satan over him and man's own utter helplessness; the problem of sin, enmity, hatred, pride, selfishness, warfare, death, etc. It is like a mountainous argument built up for God to answer. They are sure that He can do it, but there is breathless suspense as to *how* He will do it. They behold the Church as the vessel in which He will give the answer. The components of the Church are humanly as manifold and diverse in dispositions, temperaments, natures, and propensities as there are persons. In them by nature are found all the results and effects of the Fall. Then *grace* gets to work; calls them, chooses them, saves them, sanctifies them, and changes them so that they go altogether " contrary to nature." They no longer do what they used to do. They do what they never would have done. This is operating and developing every day. Grace, grace, grace ! The word occurs a dozen times in " Ephesians," and its glorious issue is that " in the ages to come he might show the exceeding riches of his grace . . . toward us in Christ Jesus " (ii. 7). So the Church and its members pass into every kind of trial and testing—persecution, reproach, adversity, sorrow, loneliness, disappointment, physical suffering, frustration, etc.—and the reactions through the grace of God are quite other than they would be apart from it.

There, where things are known for their eternal value and right meaning, this " manifold wisdom of God " is causing principalities and powers to worship and glorify God. And because the Church serves Him in this way it is destined to share His glory, and come down " out of heaven . . . having the glory of God." It can be easily seen how the Cross relates to this. Initially it secures for God the vessel. Progressively as a principle it empowers to put aside all that works against His glory. The Cross lies at the heart of every disappointment triumphantly borne, and every adversity meekly endured.

Because of the great solution which the Cross is to the problem which has filled the universe, angels and archangels and all the host of heaven adore Him Who thought of it—Whose unsearchable wisdom found expression in " *Jesus Christ and him crucified.*"

INSPIRATIONAL LIBRARY

Beautiful purse / pocket size editions of Christian Classics bound in flexible leatherette or genuine Bonded Leather. The Bonded Leather editions have gold edges and make beautiful gifts.

THE BIBLE PROMISE BOOK   Over 1000 promises from God's Word arranged by topic. What does the Bible promise about matters like: Anger, Illness, Jealousy, Sex, Money, Old Age, et cetera, et cetera.

Flexible Leatherette . . . . **$ 3.95**
Genuine Bonded Leather **$10.95**

DAILY LIGHT   One of the most popular daily devotionals with readings for both morning and evening. One page for each day of the year.

Flexible Leatherette . . . . **$ 3.95**
Genuine Bonded Leather **$10.95**

WISDOM FROM THE BIBLE   Daily thoughts from the Proverbs which communicate truth about ourselves and the world around us. One page for each day in the year.

Flexible Leatherette . . . . **$ 3.95**
Genuine Bonded Leather **$10.95**

MY DAILY PRAYER JOURNAL   Each page is dated and has a Scripture verse and ample room for you to record your thoughts, prayers and praises. One page for each day of the year.

Flexible Leatherette . . . . **$ 3.95**
Genuine Bonded Leather **$10.95**

Available wherever books are sold.

or order from:
Barbour and Company, Inc.
164 Mill Street   Box 1219
Westwood, New Jersey   07675

If you order by mail add $1.00 to your order for shipping.